W9-CHP-350

Conure

2nd Edition

Julie Rach Mancini

Howell
Book House™

Copyright © 2006 by Wiley Publishing, Inc., Hoboken, New Jersey. All rights reserved.

Howell Book House
Published by Wiley Publishing, Inc., Hoboken, New Jersey

For general information on our other products and services or to obtain technical support please contact our Customer Care Department within the U.S. at (800) 762-2974, outside the U.S. at (317) 572-3993 or fax (317) 572-4002.

Wiley also publishes its books in a variety of electronic formats. Some content that appears in print may not be available in electronic books. For more information about Wiley products, please visit our web site at www.wiley.com.

Library of Congress Cataloging-in-Publication Data:
Mancini, Julie R. (Julie Rach)
    Conure / Julie Rach Mancini.— 2nd ed.
        p. cm. — (Your happy healthy pet)
    ISBN-13: 978-0-471-74714-7 (cloth)
    ISBN-10: 0-471-74714-9 (cloth)
    1. Conures. I. Title. II. Owner's guide to a happy healthy pet.
SF473.C65R335 2006
636.6'865—dc22
                                                    2005031024

Printed in the United States of America

10   9   8   7   6   5   4   3   2   1

2nd Edition

Book design by Melissa Auciello-Brogan
Cover design by Michael J. Freeland
Book production by Wiley Publishing, Inc. Composition Services

About the Author

Birds have been an important part of Julie Rach Mancini's life ever since her father built a window shelf to feed pigeons as mealtime entertainment for her when she was a toddler. Her parents got her first bird, a parakeet named Charlie, when she was six, and she kept a special African grey parrot named Sindbad for more than ten years. Professionally, her interest in birds began to combine with her love of writing when the editors of *Pet Health News* asked her to write about bird health in 1988. She assisted in the preparation of the first issue of *Birds USA*, a successful annual publication aimed at the first-time pet bird owner, and became managing editor, and then editor, of *Bird Talk* in 1992. Julie has been a freelance writer since 1997, with pets as her primary focus.

About Howell Book House

Since 1961, Howell Book House has been America's premier publisher of pet books. We're dedicated to companion animals and the people who love them, and our books reflect that commitment. Our stable of authors—training experts, veterinarians, breeders, and other authorities—is second to none. And we've won more Maxwell Awards from the Dog Writers Association of America than any other publisher.

As we head toward the half-century mark, we're more committed than ever to providing new and innovative books, along with the classics our readers have grown to love. This year, we're launching several exciting new initiatives, including redesigning the Howell Book House logo and revamping our biggest pet series, Your Happy Healthy Pet™, with bold new covers and updated content. From bringing home a new puppy to competing in advanced equestrian events, Howell has the titles that keep animal lovers coming back again and again.

Contents

Shopping List

You'll need to do a bit of stocking up before you bring your new bird home. Below is a basic list of some must-have supplies. For more detailed information on the selection of each item, consult chapter 5. For specific guidance on what grooming tools you'll need, review chapter 7.

- ☐ Cage
- ☐ Open food and water bowls (at least two sets of each for easier dish changing and cage cleaning)
- ☐ Perches of various diameters and materials
- ☐ Sturdy scrub brush to clean the perches
- ☐ Food (a good quality fresh seed mixture or a formulated diet, such as pellets or crumbles)

- ☐ Powdered vitamin and mineral supplement to sprinkle on your pet's fresh foods
- ☐ A variety of safe, fun toys
- ☐ Cage cover (an old sheet or towel with no holes or ravels will serve this purpose nicely)
- ☐ Playgym (to give your conure time out of his cage and a place to exercise)

You're likely to be dying to pick up a few other items before bringing your bird home. Use the following blanks to note any additional items you'll be shopping for.

- ☐ _____
- ☐ _____
- ☐ _____
- ☐ _____
- ☐ _____
- ☐ _____
- ☐ _____
- ☐ _____
- ☐ _____
- ☐ _____

Pet Sitter's Guide

We can be reached at (___)_____-_____ Cellphone (___)_____-_____

We will return on _____ (date) at _____ (approximate time)

Bird's Name _____

Species, Age, and Sex _____

Important Names and Numbers

Vet's Name _____ Phone (___)_____-_____

Address_____

Emergency Vet's Name _____ Phone (___)_____-_____

Address_____

Poison Control _____ (or call vet first)

Other individual to contact in case of emergency _____

Care Instructions

In the following three blanks let the sitter know what to feed, how much, and when; when to give treats; and when and how to exercise the bird.

Morning_____

Afternoon_____

Evening _____

Medications needed (dosage and schedule) _____

Any special medical conditions_____

Grooming instructions _____

My bird's favorite playtime activities, quirks, and other tips _____

Part I

The World
of the Conure

The Conure

Nare

Crown

Cere

Nape

Beak

Mantle

Breast

Flight Feathers

Rump

Tail Feathers

Chapter 1

What Is a Conure?

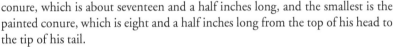

Conures are New World parrots, which means they are native to the Americas. They were first found throughout Latin America, from Mexico through the islands of the Caribbean to southern Chile. The largest conure is the Patagonian conure, which is about seventeen and a half inches long, and the smallest is the painted conure, which is eight and a half inches long from the top of his head to the tip of his tail.

Conures' native environments include a wide variety of climates and terrains, from savannahs to tropical forests and cooler mountain areas. They are peaceful birds who live in large flocks. Conures' nesting sites in the wild range from niches carved into sandstone cliffs to tree cavities.

Some species, such as the red throat, olive throat, Cuban, and peach front, nest in active termite mounds or termite nests in trees. To do this, the birds break into the termite mound with their beaks and dig a tunnel and a nesting chamber. This effort takes them about a week, after which they leave the nest alone for a week so the termites can seal off the nest from the rest of the mound. The birds then return and set up housekeeping.

In the wild, conures eat a variety of foods, including grass seeds, fruits, cactus, berries, nuts, flowers, insects, and grains. They can also do damage to cultivated crops, which makes them unpopular with farmers in their native habitats.

The First Documented Conures

Conures were first described in literature in 1724 by Jean Baptiste Labat, a French priest who spent thirteen years as a missionary in the colonies of the West Indies. While there, he also studied and documented many of the native species of plants and animals he saw. Labat described and drew pictures of a species of bird he called *Aratinga labati* on the island of Guadaloupe. Some naturalists believe this green parrot with a few red head feathers may have been a captive Cuban conure *(Aratinga euops)*, or he may be a now-extinct species.

Conures began to be imported into Europe and the United States more than a hundred years ago, and a few species, such as the green conure, were being bred in the United States in the mid-1930s. Unfortunately, at the time most people believed it was easier to go into the jungle and capture wild birds, rather than setting up the birds they had in breeding colonies. With habitat destruction and the increased demand for birds in the pet trade, this situation had to change.

Domestic Breeding Begins

The brightly colored sun and jenday conures spurred aviculturists into breeding conures on a large scale. The sun conure was first imported into the United States in the 1960s, and these birds were routinely bred in captivity by the

There are many conure species. This is a jenday conure on the left with two gold crown babies.

What's in a Name?

The conure's common name comes from the old scientific name for the genus conures belong to: *Conorus*—from the Greek words *cone* (cone) and *ourus* (tail-bearing). That genus is now known as *Aratinga* (meaning "little macaw"). The genus name is the first part of the scientific name assigned to every species of plant and animal. It shows what larger group this individual belongs to. The *Aratinga* group, for example, includes many types of parakeets.

The scientific name is important because the common name for an animal can vary from country to country and even within a country, causing a great deal of confusion. When the scientific name is used, everyone knows exactly which bird you are talking about.

1980s. The jenday conure soon followed. After that, aviculturists turned their attention to other conure species, which turned out to be a benefit for both pet owners and wild conures. Pet owners received more suitable companion birds when domestic-bred conures were available, and wild conures were less threatened with trapping and exportation because the demand for them decreased.

Although wild-caught birds were still fairly common pets into the early 1980s, most conures offered for sale as pets are now domestically-bred birds. This means they are healthier and better suited emotionally to be pets than the wild-caught birds of twenty or twenty-five years ago.

Many Conure Species

Depending on which expert you consult, between forty-five and one hundred different species and subspecies of birds in six genera make up the group of parrots we call conures. This book does not include all of the different species because not all are commonly kept as pets.

This book focuses primarily on the *Aratinga* (pronounced *ah-rah-ting-ah*) and *Pyrrhura* (pronounced *py-hurrah*) genera, which include the most common pets.

A Link to Dinosaurs?

In 2001, scientists announced that a 130-million-year-old feathered dinosaur fossil had been discovered in China. It was the first dinosaur found with its body covering intact, and it was identified as a Dromaeosaur, a small, fast-running dinosaur closely related to Velociraptor, with a sickle claw on the middle toe and stiffening rods in the tail. According to the American Museum of Natural History, Dromaeosaurs were advanced theropods, which is a group of two-legged predators that includes Tyrannosaurus rex. Dromoaesaurs had sharp teeth and bones that were very similar to those of modern-day birds.

The fossil was found in Liaoning Province in northeastern China. It was described as looking like a large duck with a long tail. The animal's head and tail were covered with downy fibers, and it had other featherlike structures on the back of its arms and on other parts of its body.

The first feathered dinosaur was found in China in 1995. This discovery, Sinosauropteryx, was also a theropod dinosaur, and it

A few birds in other genera, such as *Nandayus*, *Cyanoliseus*, and *Enicognathus*, are discussed as well because they also make good pets.

One way to distinguish the two genera of conures is to remember that *Aratinga* birds are brightly colored (vibrant greens and reds, for example), while *Pyrrhura* birds are darker in coloration (deep green or maroon). *Aratinga* birds also lack the light-colored markings on the upper chest that *Pyrrhura* birds characteristically have.

Some breeders think conures and macaws are closely related. In fact, the genus name *Aratinga* means "little macaw." There are some physical similarities worth noting: similar body shapes, brightly colored feathers, and

For an in-depth look at the many species of conures, consult Joseph Forshaw's *Parrots of the World*, which describes the appearance, native habitat, and natural history of each species in detail.

was also found in Liaoning Province. Sinosauropteryx dates from between 121 and 135 million years ago, and it falls in between Archaeopteryx, the earliest known bird, which lived about 150 million years ago, and Protarchaeopteryx robusta, which lived at about the same time as Sinosauropteryx but probably could not fly, despite the presence of feathers on its body.

Several other species of feathered dinosaurs have been found in the same region, and scientists believe that some species of dinosaurs developed feathers to help them keep warm.

Fossils of birdlike dinosaurs and dinosaurlike birds have been found in Madagascar, Mongolia, and Patagonia, as well as in China. The Eoalulavis, found in Spain, was one of the earliest birds that could maneuver well during flight, thanks to a feather tuft on its thumb called an alula. This feature is found on birds today, and it helps them with takeoffs and landings. Some scientists theorize that birds evolved from dinosaurs, while others are still seeking an earlier reptile ancestor for birds.

long tails. Further genetic analysis is needed to determine just how close the relationship is between these groups of birds.

Conure Characteristics

Conures are outgoing, cheerful, inquisitive little acrobats who take an active interest in their surroundings and the activities of their human family. They are also intelligent, playful, and extremely affectionate.

Although they are smaller members of the parrot family, conures have large personalities and sometimes seem to be unaware of or unable to remember their size. To prevent tragic consequences and an emergency trip to the veterinary hospital, conure owners should closely supervise all interactions between these birds and other pets, such as larger parrots, dogs, and cats.

Birds are more closely linked to dinosaurs than this iguana is. Without the feathers on these babies, you can see the resemblance.

Conures offer something for almost anyone. Some species are known to be cuddly, others can learn to talk fairly well, and still others are strikingly beautiful. Most are also quite affordable pets. (Chapter 2, "All Types of Conures," describes the twenty-five most popular species.)

Strange Sleeping Habits

Another interesting aspect of the conure personality is their tendency to snuggle under something when they sleep. Don't be surprised to find your bird under a corner of his cage paper if the cage he lives in doesn't have a grille to keep the bird out of the cage tray. You can provide your conure with a washcloth, a fuzzy toy, or something else cuddly to snuggle with.

Don't become alarmed the first time you see your conure asleep with his head tucked under his wing and resting on one leg. Although it seems your bird has lost his head or a leg, he's fine. Sleeping on one foot with his head tucked under his wing (actually with his head turned about 180 degrees and his beak tucked into the feathers on the back of his neck) is a normal sleeping position for many parrots,

> *Aratinga* conures are noted for their loud, strident calls, as well as their lively, fun-loving, playful, cheerful personalities.

although it looks a bit unusual or uncomfortable to bird owners. Be aware, too, that your bird will occasionally perch on one leg while resting the other.

Conures also fall asleep in their food bowls, often on their backs with their feet in the air. You may fear your bird has died the first time you see him do this. But some conures routinely sleep on their backs. As long as he appears healthy, eats well, and acts normally, you have no cause for concern if your conure sleeps on his back. Some parent birds even feed their chicks when the babies are lying on their backs, so it's a perfectly comfortable position for a conure to be in.

Some conure species are known to be extra cuddly.

Bath Time

Conures are also great bathers. They'll try to bathe in their water bowls if nothing else is available, but they really prefer to be dunked under the water faucet or to stand under a light shower in the kitchen sink. Be sure the water is lukewarm before letting your conure take a quick dip, and allow plenty of time for your bird's feathers to dry before he goes to bed (a blow dryer set on low can accelerate the drying process).

Escape Artists

Finally, conures can be excellent escape artists, so make sure the cage you select for your conure is completely secure and that the door and cage grille are not prone to popping open or falling out. Make sure the food and water bowl openings have covers that you can slide into place to help keep your pet in his cage while you're changing the bowls. Check to make sure all windows in your home have screens on them and doors to the outside world are closed tightly before you let your conure out of his cage.

Chapter 2

All Types of Conures

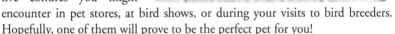

Here, in alphabetical order, are twenty-five conures you might encounter in pet stores, at bird shows, or during your visits to bird breeders. Hopefully, one of them will prove to be the perfect pet for you!

In the descriptions that follow, the scientific names are provided to help you distinguish between the species. Some books classify conures by their common North American names, while others call them by their common British names. But the scientific names are the same no matter where in the world you go, so they will assist you in determining which conure is which.

Austral Conure

(Enicognathus ferrugineus)

In her native habitat of southern Chile, the austral conure has the distinction of being the southernmost parrot in the wild. She measures fourteen and a half inches long and weighs about five ounces. Australs were exported to Europe and the United States for more than 100 years, but they failed to catch on with breeders because of their dull coloration, so they might be difficult to find.

In captivity, these olive drab birds with black beaks, gray feet, and blackish-gray eye rings make quite good pets. They are less noisy than most conures, but they tend to vocalize in the evening.

Australs like to forage on the floor of their cage or aviary, looking for tubers, nuts, seeds, berries, and leaf buds. Although in general, bird owners should be concerned if they see their bird on the bottom of her cage all the time, this is perfectly normal behavior for an Austral conure and no cause for alarm. Austral owners do need to pay extra attention to the cleanliness of their pet's cage floor, however, because their bird will be spending more time down there than other species might.

Austral conures are generally less noisy than most conures, but they do tend to vocalize in the evening.

Aztec Conure

(Aratinga nana astec)

This conure, which many consider to be a subspecies of the olive-throated conure, has green head feathers and olive-colored body feathers. Her beak is horn-colored and her feet are gray. Aztecs measure about ten inches long and weigh about three ounces. Their native range is from central Mexico to western Panama.

As pets, Aztecs are known for their talking ability, which is considered quite good for a conure. They are feisty little birds who charm everyone they meet. Somewhat rare as pets, they are worth the wait if you are looking for a small bird with a big personality.

Black-Capped Conure

(Pyrrhura rupicola)

This uncommon conure has a black forehead, dark brown chest feathers that are scalloped in off-white, green belly feathers, and red feathers on the leading edge of her wings. The beak is gray and the legs are dark gray. The black-cap measures about ten inches long and weighs about three ounces.

Black-caps were imported into the United States from southeastern Peru, northern Bolivia, and northwestern Brazil in extremely small numbers in the early 1980s. However, that small number of birds bred prolifically, so this little conure is now available as a pet.

Blue-Crown Conure

(Aratinga acuticaudata)

As her name suggests, the blue-crown has a blue head and blue facial feathers. The coloring becomes more intense as the bird matures. Her body feathers are

primarily green, the undersides of her wings are yellowish-green, and her tail feathers have reddish undersides. This bird has a horn-colored beak, white eye rings that are featherless, and pinkish feet.

Blue-crowns measure about fourteen and a half inches long and weigh about seven ounces. They were first bred in captivity in Great Britain in the early 1970s. In the wild, they are found in South America, from Venezuela to Argentina.

Blue-crowns, which are sometimes called *sharp-tailed conures*, can be noisy (especially if they are surprised or excited), but they are reasonably peaceful birds. They are popular as pets. They have the ability to talk and have friendly personalities.

Blue-crown conures can be noisy birds.

Brown-Throated Conure

(Aratinga pertinax)

This uncommon little conure has an orangish face, green wing and body feathers, buff-colored eye rings, a black beak, and gray legs. She measures about nine and a half inches long and weighs about four ounces. She was imported into St. Thomas in the Virgin Islands about 125 years ago and is sometimes called the St. Thomas conure. She is also found in Central and South America, from Panama to Brazil. There are fourteen recognized subspecies of this conure, which may also be called the orange-cheek or the brown-ear.

Some conure fanciers believe brown-throats make great pets, while others are quick to point out that these birds can be aggressive, destructive, and noisy. As with all creatures, each brown-throat has her own personality. To determine whether she's the right bird for you, spend some time with a brown-throated conure before making a decision to own one.

Spend some time with a brown-throated conure before you decide to own one.

Cactus Conure

(Aratinga cactorum)

These conures from northeastern Brazil have a gray forehead and throat feathers, a yellowish belly, and green wings. Their beaks are horn colored, their eye rings are white, and their feet are black. Cactus conures measure about ten inches long and weigh about three ounces. The bird's common name comes from the fact that cactus fruit comprises a large part of her diet.

Cactus conures can become affectionate pets. They are easily tamed, are not destructive, and tend to be quieter than some other conures. Unfortunately, Brazil did not export many of these birds, so these little charmers are not common as pets. Some breeders are starting to raise them in captivity.

Cherry-Headed Conure

(Aratinga erythrogenys)

Sometimes called the red-headed or red-masked conure, mature cherry-heads have red facial feathers; green body feathers with a sprinkling of red on the

throat, shoulders, and thighs; bare white eye rings; horn-colored beaks; and dark gray legs. Mature cherry-heads are about thirteen inches long and weigh between five and seven ounces.

Young cherry-heads are predominantly green until their first molts, and older birds can take up to ten years to fully develop their red plumage. In the wild, cherry-heads are found in a narrow range in western Ecuador and Peru.

Cherry-heads can learn to talk, and if they do, they often opt to speak their owners' language instead of vocalizing in conure speech. Cherry-heads are popular as pets.

Cherry-heads can take up to ten years to fully develop their red plumage.

Dusky Conure

(Aratinga weddelli)

Sweetness seems to be a hallmark of this commonly kept small conure, which is sometimes called Weddell's conure. Other adjectives used to describe her include calm, gentle, and mellow. She is not an eye-catching bird, being mostly green with a gray-blue head, white eye rings, and a black beak and feet, but her affectionate personality soon wins hearts. Conure fanciers routinely describe her as quiet, which is not an adjective often used to describe a conure. A dusky conure can also learn to talk, which may win her even more fans.

Duskies measure about eleven inches long and weigh about four ounces. In the wild, they are found from southeastern Colombia to western Brazil.

Finsch's Conure
(Aratinga finschi)

These popular pet birds bear a striking resemblance to the red-fronted, or Wagler's conure, but Finsch's conures have red feathers on the front edges of their wings. Their body feathers are mostly green, their beaks are horn colored, their eye rings are creamy white, and they have gray-brown legs and feet. Mature Finsch's conures measure about eleven inches long and weigh about six ounces.

As with the cherry-heads, young Finsch's conures are completely green. As they mature, they develop their characteristic red foreheads. The native range for the Finsch's conure is southern Nicaragua to western Panama.

Gold-Capped Conure
(Aratinga auricapilla)

This commonly kept conure has a golden-orange forehead, a green chest, and a reddish belly. Her eye rings are white, her beak is gray-black, and her legs are gray. The gold-cap measures about twelve inches long and weighs about five ounces. She is a common pet bird in the United States.

Gold-caps, sometimes called golden-headed conures, are prone to lying on their backs in their food bowls or in their owners' hands—it's simply a comfortable position for them. They are active, energetic little birds and have been captive bred in the United States since the early 1980s. Although they are not as flashy as the yellow-orange jenday or sun conures, some conure experts believe the gold-cap makes the least amount of noise and has the best pet potential of this golden trio.

Because her rainforest habitat is decreasing, the gold-cap is now rare in her native range, which is southeastern Brazil.

Green-Cheeked Conure
(Pyrrhura molinae)

Sometimes the green-cheeked and the maroon-bellied conures are confused with each other. Although recent DNA analysis suggests they may, in fact, be the same species, I will nonetheless treat them separately. The green-cheeked

Green-cheeked conures are bold, inquisitive, and loud.

conure and the maroon-bellied are both popular pets, and they do resemble each other quite closely: Both birds have brown heads, green cheek feathers, brown chest feathers scalloped with buff or yellow, maroon belly and tail feathers, white eye rings, gray beaks, and dark gray legs. But the green-cheeked has a darker brown head, less maroon on her belly, more green on her cheeks, and a lighter background on the barred area on the chest feathers. The green-cheeked also has a completely maroon tail.

In the wild, the green-cheeked is found in west central Brazil, northern Bolivia, and northwestern Argentina. She measures about ten inches long and weighs about four ounces. Green-cheeks make engaging, bold, and inquisitive pets. They lack the loud voice of an *Aratinga,* so their vocalizations should be tolerable for most owners.

Half-Moon Conure

(Aratinga canicularis)

The half-moon, or Petz's conure, is often confused with the peach-fronted conure. Half-moon conures have orange foreheads, olive chest feathers, green wing and belly feathers, horn-colored beaks (as opposed to the peach-front's black beak), orange-yellow eye rings (the peach-front's eye ring has small orange feathers on it), and dark gray feet. Half-moons measure nine and a half inches long and weigh about two and a half ounces.

The half-moon conure may be the best known of the *Aratinga* species because she was widely imported from western Central America for a number of years. Since the 1970s, half-moons have been bred in captivity in the United States.

Young half-moons are as bold as brass. These fearless birds can learn to talk, and they make tame, affectionate pets.

Jenday Conure

(Aratinga jandaya)

Almost as colorful as the sun conure, the jenday is an eye-catching bird. She has predominantly orange-red body feathers, green wings with blue accent feathers, white eye rings, a black beak, and blackish feet. Jendays measure about twelve inches long and weigh about five ounces.

These half-moon conures are fearless!

This native of northeastern Brazil has not been imported into the United States since the early 1980s; breeders have been able to meet the needs of pet owners with domestically bred birds. Although they can be somewhat noisy, jendays make inquisitive, acrobatic pets.

Maroon-Bellied Conure

(Pyrrhura frontalis)

Like her green-cheeked relative, the maroon-bellied conure has a brown head, green cheek feathers, brown chest feathers scalloped with buff or yellow, a maroon belly and tail feathers, white eye rings, a gray beak, and dark gray legs. In contrast to the green-cheeked, the maroon-bellied, as her name suggests, has a larger patch of maroon belly feathers, more yellow on her chest, and green head feathers. Maroon-bellieds measure about ten inches long and weigh about three ounces.

Maroon-bellieds, which may also be called scaly-breasted conures, were imported into the United States and Europe from their native ranges in southeastern Brazil, Uruguay, Paraguay, and northern Argentina starting in the 1920s. The species has since been set up in captive breeding programs, and pairs have done quite well producing chicks.

Maroon-bellieds have large personalities in their small bodies, and they make lively, playful pets.

Maroon-Tailed Conure

(Pyrrhura melanura)

This bird also goes by the name black-tailed conure. She measures about nine and a half inches long and weighs about three ounces. The maroon-tailed has a brown forehead; green cheeks, wing and belly feathers; and brown-green chest feathers that are scalloped with white. The maroon-tailed also has red feathers on the leading edges of her wings. Her eye rings are white and her beak and feet are gray. As you might expect, her tail feathers are black on top and maroon on the underside, which gives rise to both of her common names.

In the wild, maroon-tailed conures are found from southern Venezuela to northeastern Peru. Maroon-taileds make entertaining pets, and they are not hard to find. They enjoy being around people and take to strangers rather quickly, winning new friends with their charming personalities.

Mitred Conure

(Aratinga mitrata)

Mitred conures are primarily green with reddish foreheads, creamy white eye rings, horn-colored beaks, and brown legs. As with other green and red conures discussed here, young mitreds are completely green until their first molt, when the red forehead starts to become evident. Mitreds are fifteen inches long and weigh about eight and a half ounces.

Mitred conures can be very affectionate, but they're also loud.

Mitreds became well known to pet owners when importing birds was at its height; thousands of these parrots were brought into the United States from the mitred's native habitat, which stretches from central Peru to northwestern Argentina. Their popularity is even greater with the introduction of domestically bred birds.

Although mitreds can be quite vocal, they are also very affectionate pets. This loyal affection for their owners has won the species many fans over the years. They also like to chew, so be sure your mitred has lots of toys she can destroy.

Nanday Conure

(Nandayus nenday)

One of the more colorful conure species, the nanday has a black forehead and cheeks, bluish throat, green belly and wing feathers, orange leg feathers, white eye rings, black beak, and pink feet. Nandays, which are also known as black-headed or black-masked conures, are twelve inches long and weigh about five ounces.

Nandays were exported from their native habitat, which ranges

Domestically bred nanday conures are naturally social birds who thrive on attention from you.

from southeastern Bolivia to northern Argentina, for more than a hundred years. As is the case with many wild-caught parrots, wild nandays developed a reputation as poor pets. Today's hand-fed, domestically bred nandays, however, are difficult to top. They are naturally social birds who thrive on attention from their owners, and they get along well with other parrots. The nanday's main drawback as a pet is that some of them can be quite loud, so they may not be well-suited for life in an apartment or a town house.

It's difficult to be indifferent about a nanday because these acrobatic little extroverts quickly charm their way into your heart. Many nanday owners are extremely loyal to their colorful little friends. First-time owners need to remember that nandays tend to fall asleep on their backs with their feet in the air—a behavior that can be alarming the first time you see it.

Patagonian Conure

(Cyanoliseus patagonus)

This is the largest conure, measuring about seventeen and a half inches long and weighing a little more than half a pound. Although some might describe their plumage as dull, Patis are actually quite colorful with their olive heads, orange and yellow bellies, blue flight feathers, pink feet, black beaks, and white eye rings. The natural range for this conure is central Chile, northern and central Argentina, and southern Uruguay.

In the wild, Patagonians are known to be ground feeders, so don't be alarmed if your Pati spends a lot of time on the bottom of her cage. As long as the bird appears otherwise healthy, this is a natural behavior. Patis are quite cuddly pets and some can become good talkers. They have bred readily in captivity and are not hard to find. Among the drawbacks to keeping these conures are the facts that they can be quite loud, they require large cages to be comfortable, and they are voracious chewers.

Peach-Fronted Conure

(Aratinga aurea)

Sometimes called the golden-crowned conure, the peach-fronted conure can be easily confused with the half-moon. Peach-fronts have deep orange foreheads,

olive throats, yellow belly feathers, and green wing feathers. Their beaks and feet are black, and their eye rings are covered with small orange feathers.

The peach-fronted occupies a wide range—southern Brazil to northern Argentina—in her native habitat. She measures about ten inches long and weighs about four ounces.

Peach-fronted conures have been kept by bird owners and breeders for more than a hundred years. As pets, these conures have fairly good talking abilities and sweet dispositions. However, they can be destructive, noisy, and aggressive toward other parrots during the breeding season.

Peach-fronted conures have been kept as pets for more than 100 years.

Queen of Bavaria Conure

(Aratinga guarouba)

The Queen of Bavaria is a large, visually striking bird. Her primary feather color is brilliant yellow with olive green flight feathers, and she has a horn-colored beak, white eye rings, and pinkish feet. Queens measure about fourteen inches long and weigh about half a pound. Because they are so eye-catching, they have been featured in advertisements for premium bird foods. The San Diego Zoo has a pair of Queens on display that I make a point of visiting each time I'm there. These large conures cause more than a few visitors to stop and take a second look.

Queens, which are sometimes called golden conures, are native to a small area in northeastern Brazil. They are endangered in the wild because of deforestation, nest site destruction, and human encroachment. They have a long history of captive breeding that dates from 1939 in Sri Lanka. This species has been bred in the United States for more than fifty years. Despite this long history in captivity, Queens are uncommon pets, and they command top dollar.

Queens are prone to a few behavioral problems, including loud vocalization, feather picking, and aggression toward other parrots, particularly during breeding season. However, they are generally tame and affectionate toward their owners. This species is not recommended for first-time conure owners because they require a great deal of attention and because they are still not common in aviculture.

Queen of Bavaria conures are big, affectionate birds. However, they are also prone to behavior problems and are not a good choice for the first-time bird owner.

Red-Fronted Conure

(Aratinga wagleri)

Also known as Wagler's conure, the red-fronted is a green bird with a red forehead, white eye rings, a horn-colored beak, and brownish feet. Young birds start out life completely green and develop their red foreheads as they mature. The red-fronted is about fourteen and a half inches long and weighs about six and a half ounces.

In the wild, the red-fronted conure's native range stretches in a narrow band from northern Venezuela to southern Peru. These birds have been bred in captivity in the United States since 1957. They make entertaining pets and are capable of learning a variety of tricks.

Red-Throated Conure

(Aratinga holochlora rubritorquis)

This subspecies of the green conure makes a comical pet who has a good chance of becoming a talking bird. Red-throated conures measure about twelve inches long and weigh about four ounces.

In the wild, red-throateds are found from eastern Guatemala to northern Nicaragua. Across their range, these birds are highly prized as pets. They were not imported to the United States in large numbers, but the birds who are here have bred well in captivity.

Like some other types of conures, young red-throateds start out life all green (well, once they have their feathers, anyway). They develop their red throats after their first molt. Red-throats also have beige eye rings, horn-colored beaks, and brownish legs.

Red-throated conures don't develop their red feathers until after their first molt.

Slender-Billed Conure
(Enicognathus leptorhynchus)

Like the austral, this olive drab conure with gray eye rings, a reddish stripe of feathers around her eyes, a black beak, and grayish feet has been largely overlooked in the pet trade because she simply doesn't have eye-catching plumage. This uncommon bird does, however, have an eye-catching beak that may cause some first-time bird owners to think something is wrong with her. Her upper mandible is considerably longer than that of other parrots, but it's simply an adaptation that enables the slender-billed to dig for tubers and roots in her native habitat of central Chile. The elongated bill also helps the bird retrieve one of her favorite foods—the seeds of the *Araucaria araucana* tree. Slender-billed conures kept in captivity might appreciate pine nuts, which are similar to their favorite wild seeds.

Slender-billed conures, which are sometimes called long-billed conures, are one of the larger conures, measuring about sixteen inches long and weighing about six ounces. They are peaceful birds who do well in captivity. They can be quite noisy when they want to be, but they can also learn to talk rather well.

Slender-billeds tend to spend long periods of time on the cage floor, foraging for food, so don't be alarmed if your slender-billed seems to be down in her cage bottom all the time. You can make the hunt for food more interesting for this bird

Slender-billed conures like to forage for food on the cage floor.

by scattering a few seeds in the bottom of her cage. Be alert to the condition of the cage bottom and keep it scrupulously clean to help ensure the health of your conure.

Sun Conure

(Aratinga solstitialis)

These flashy little birds have been described as the Cadillacs of the conure group. A mature sun conure (pictured on the first page of this chapter) is a brilliant blaze of orange, yellow, red, and green feathers, and younger sun conures have mottled green plumage until their first molt. Mature suns have black beaks, white eye rings, and grayish feet. They measure about twelve inches long and weigh about four and a half ounces.

Suns are found in the wild from Guyana to northeastern Brazil, but they have been captive bred in the United States for many years. As pets, they are known for being content to be with their owners for hours at a time, sitting on a shoulder or the back of a chair. They can be noisy if ignored but otherwise make fine pets.

White-Eyed Conure

(Aratinga leucophthalmus)

White-eyed conures take their name from the bare ring of white skin around their eyes. They are predominantly green birds with a sprinkling of red on their bodies, horn-colored beaks, and gray-brown legs. White-eyed conures measure about thirteen inches long and weigh about four and a half ounces.

In the wild, white-eyed conures can be found from Guyana to Uruguay. They have bred well in captivity and are commonly available as pets. They can be quite affectionate, engaging birds and may learn to talk at a quite early age.

White-eyed conures are affectionate birds and may learn to talk when they are still quite young.

Chapter 3

Choosing the Right Conure for You

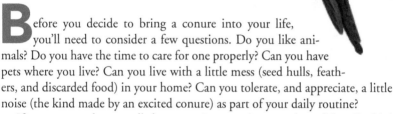

Before you decide to bring a conure into your life, you'll need to consider a few questions. Do you like animals? Do you have the time to care for one properly? Can you have pets where you live? Can you live with a little mess (seed hulls, feathers, and discarded food) in your home? Can you tolerate, and appreciate, a little noise (the kind made by an excited conure) as part of your daily routine?

If you answered yes to all these questions, you're a good candidate for bird ownership. Your next question might be, "Why do I want a bird?" Here are some of the answers.

Why Choose a Bird?

Birds' small size makes them good pets for today's smaller living spaces. More of us are living in apartments, mobile or manufactured homes, or condominiums, which makes it awkward and inconvenient to keep a large pet who needs a yard and lots of regular exercise. Birds just seem to fit better in apartments, condos, mobile homes, and other smaller living spaces.

If you're a bird owner who rents an apartment or a house, you may be able to get your current landlord to write a letter of reference for your birds that you can use to show future landlords, explaining how responsible you are as a bird owner

Birds are really smart and crave your company and attention.

and how well behaved your bird has been. In many rental leases, birds may not even be considered pets because they are kept in a cage much of the time. This means you may be able to keep them without having to surrender a sizable security deposit to your landlord.

Birds interact well with their owners. Although a bird isn't as blindly loyal as the average dog, he is far more interactive than a fish, a hamster, or even a guinea pig. As an added bonus, many birds can learn to whistle or talk, which is unique among pets and which many bird owners find amusing and entertaining.

Birds require consistent, but not constant, attention. This can be a plus for today's busy single people and families. Although birds can't be ignored all day, they are content to entertain themselves for part of the day while their owners are busy elsewhere.

The needs and companionship of a bird provide a reason to get up in the morning. The value of this cannot be overestimated for older bird owners and single people who are on their own. Birds provide all the benefits of the human-animal bond, including lower blood pressure and reduced levels of stress.

Finally, birds are intelligent pets. Whoever coined the phrase "birdbrain" didn't appreciate how smart some birds are. On intelligence tests, some larger parrots have scored at levels comparable to chimpanzees, dolphins, and preschool-age children.

Where Will You Get Your Conure?

You can get your conure from bird breeders, who will advertise in bird specialty magazines and in the pet section of your newspaper's classified ads, at bird shows, or from bird specialty stores. Let's look at each in a bit more detail.

Classified Ads

Classified ads are usually placed by private parties. If the advertiser offers young birds, you've found a private breeder who wants to place a few birds in good homes. Most pet conures can leave the breeder's home at around 3 months of age. Some breeders may also offer older birds for sale from time to time. These are most likely breeder birds who are too old to produce chicks but who would still make good pets.

Bird Shows

Shows offer bird breeders and bird buyers an opportunity to get together to share a love for birds. Bird shows can give you the chance to see many different types of birds all in one place, which can help you narrow your choices if you're undecided about which species to keep. At a bird show, you can watch to see which birds win consistently and then talk to the breeder of these birds after the show to see if they expect any chicks.

Bird Specialty Stores

Specialty stores might be the ideal place to purchase a conure. If a store in your area sells conures, you'll need to visit and make sure it's clean and well kept. Walk around the store a bit. Do the cages look and smell like they're cleaned regularly? Do the birds in the cages appear to be alert, well fed, and healthy? Do the cages appear crowded or do the animals inside have some room to move around?

Look at the birds available for sale. If possible, sit down and watch them for a while. Don't rush this important step. Do some of them seem bolder than the others? Consider those first, because you want a curious, active, robust pet, rather than a shy animal who hides in a corner.

You may think that saving a small, picked-upon conure from

A curious, active bird is more likely to be a good companion.

What Does the Band Mean?

Leg bands on birds help identify a particular breeder's stock. They can also help establish an age for your bird, since many of them have the year of hatch as part of the band's code. And some states require that pet birds be banded with closed, traceable bands so that the origin of the bird can be determined in an effort to reduce the number of smuggled birds kept as pets in the United States.

Although bands are important for record-keeping, they also have the potential to injure your conure. If you have a particularly skittish bird and he catches his leg band on a frayed cage cover, a perch, a toy, or on part of the cage itself, your bird may panic and injure himself severely—even to the point of death—in his efforts to free himself. If your conure injures his leg, the band could further complicate the injury by cutting off the blood supply.

Although most conures can wear their leg bands successfully for their entire lives, you may want to discuss removing your bird's leg band with your avian veterinarian. If you decide to have the band removed, be sure to keep it in a safe place in case you ever have to prove that your conure was domestically raised (a necessity if you relocate abroad).

his cagemates seems like the right thing to do, but please resist this urge. You want a strong, healthy, spirited bird rather than "the runt of the litter." Although it sounds hard-hearted, automatically reject any birds who are being bullied, are timid, or hide in a corner or shy away from you. It will save you some heartache in the end.

If possible, let your conure choose you. Many bird stores display their animals on T-stands or playgyms, or a breeder may bring out a clutch of babies for you to look at. If one bird waddles right up to you and wants to play, or if one comes over to check you out and just seems to want to come home with you, that's the bird for you!

The Preowned Parrot

You may see adult birds advertised for sale at a bird store or in the newspaper. Adopting an adult conure could be a great mistake if the bird has behavioral problems, or it could be the best investment you'll ever make.

People put adult conures up for sale for many reasons. Perhaps the bird detects stress in the home and begins to pull his feathers, and the owners have neither the time nor the patience to solve the problem. The owners may have a child and suddenly no longer have time for the parrot, or they may be moving and cannot take their pet with them. Some people simply lose interest in their birds and sell them after a few years.

If you want to consider a preowned parrot, make an appointment to see the bird in his current home. Ask why the owners are selling the bird and see whether you and the bird "click" on a personal level.

Ownership Challenges

An awareness of the behavioral quirks of conures will help you better prepare for them, and may help you decide whether a conure is really the right bird for you.

First, conures are noted chewers, which means they will need an abundant supply of sturdy toys that can be destroyed. If you don't provide them with proper chewing stimulation, they will find it in other places in your home, such as your entryway banister and the houseplants. Be sure to supervise your conure when he is out of his cage to prevent him from chewing on inappropriate and potentially harmful things.

Next, conures can and will vocalize, and many of them can be quite loud. Generally, members of the *Aratinga* genus of conures are louder than those of the *Pyrrhura* genus, but that's only a general rule

Make sure you buy a bird who has been hand fed and properly socialized.

Is This Conure Healthy?

Here are some of the signs that a conure is healthy. Keep them in mind when you are selecting your pet, and reject any birds who do not meet these criteria.

- Bright eyes
- Clean cere (the area above the bird's beak that covers his nares, or nostrils)
- Clean legs and vent
- Smooth feathers
- Upright posture
- Quiet breathing
- Full-chested appearance
- Bird is actively moving around the cage
- Good appetite

Remember that healthy birds spend their time doing three main activities—eating, playing, and sleeping—in about equal amounts of time. If you notice a bird who seems to only want to sleep, for instance, reject that bird in favor of another whose routine seems more balanced.

and exceptions abound. (The first part of the scientific name of the conures described in chapter 2, "All Types of Conures," tells you which genus they belong to.) To help make sure you get a relatively quiet conure, buy a hand-fed bird who has been properly socialized by the breeder. This means the breeder paid individual attention to each and every chick and took the time to handle and play with them.

If your conure seems curious about the world around him and trusting of new people, chances are very good that he was well-socialized by his breeder. You will need to continue this process by playing with your parrot and helping him explore his new environment (your home) in a safe, secure way. Once your conure comes home with you, you should give him regular periods of attention and lots of toys to play with when you aren't around. By doing this, you should be able to minimize any loud vocal outbursts.

Bringing Your Conure Home

Your new pet will need some time to adjust to his new environment, so be patient. Give your conure a chance to adjust to your family's routine gradually after you bring him home. After you set your conure up in his cage for the first time, spend a few minutes talking quietly to him, and use his name frequently while you're talking.

After a couple of days of adjustment, your conure should start to settle into his routine. You will be able to tell when your new pet has adjusted to your home, because healthy and relaxed conures will spend about equal amounts of time during the day eating, playing, sleeping, and defecating. By observation, you will soon recognize your pet's normal routine. You may also notice that your bird fluffs or shakes his feathers to greet you, or that he chirps a greeting when you uncover his cage in the morning.

Part II

Caring for Your Conure

Chapter 4

Home Sweet Home

Before you bring your feathered friend home, you have a lot of shopping to do. Selecting your conure's cage will be one of the most important decisions you make for her. You must also decide where she will live in your house or apartment. Don't wait until you bring your bird home to think this through. You'll want your new pet to settle in comfortably right away, rather than adding to her stress by relocating her several times before you decide on the right spot for the cage. Here's what you'll need to look for to set your conure up right.

Choosing a Cage

When selecting a cage for your conure, make sure the bird has room to spread her wings without touching the cage sides. Her tail should not touch the cage bottom, nor should her head brush the top. A cage that measures two feet by two feet by three feet is the minimum size for a single conure, and bigger is always better.

Check the Bars

Examine any cage you choose carefully before making your final selection. If you are choosing a cage with coated bars, make sure that the finish is not chipped, bubbled, or peeling, because your pet may find the defective spot and continue removing the finish, which can cause a cage to look old and worn before its time. Also, your pet could become ill if she ingests any of the finish.

If you are considering a galva-nized wire cage, be aware that some birds can become ill from ingesting pieces of the galvanized wire. You can prevent this "new cage syn-drome" by washing down the cage wires thoroughly with a solution of vinegar and water and then scrub-bing the cage with a wire brush to loosen any stray bits of galvanized wire. Rinse the cage thoroughly with water and let it dry before putting your bird into her new home.

Reject any cages that have sharp interior wires or wide spaces between the bars. (Recommended bar spacing for conures is about half an inch.) Sharp wires could poke your bird, she could become caught between bars that are slightly wider than recommended, or she could escape through widely spaced bars. Also be aware that birds can injure themselves on ornate scrollwork that decorates some cages. Finally, make sure the cage you choose has some horizon-tal bars in it so your conure can climb the cage walls easily for exercise.

> ## C A U T I O N
>
> ### No Bamboo
>
> If you find wooden or bamboo cages during your shopping excur-sions, reject them immediately. A busy conure beak will make short work of a wooden or bamboo cage, and you'll be left with the problem of finding a new home for your pet! These cages are designed for finches and other songbirds, who are less likely than a conure to chew on their homes.

Cage Door Options

After you've checked the overall cage quality and the bar spacing, look at the cage door. Does it open easily for you, yet remain secure enough to keep your bird in her cage when you close the door? Some conures become quite good at letting themselves out of their cage if the door does not close securely. If you dis-cover you have a feathered Houdini on your hands, a small padlock may help keep your escape artist in her place.

Will your bird's food bowl or a bowl of bath water fit through the door eas-ily? Is it long and wide enough for you to get your hand in and out of the cage comfortably—with the bird perched on your hand?

Does the door open up, down, or to the side? Some bird owners like their pets to have a play porch on a door that opens out and down, drawbridge style, while others are happy with doors that open to the side. Watch out for guillo-tine-style doors that slide up and over the cage entrance, because some conures have suffered a broken leg when the door dropped on them unexpectedly.

Cage Tray Considerations

Next, look at the tray in the bottom of the cage. Does it slide in and out of the cage easily? Remember that you will be changing the paper in this tray at least once a day for the rest of your bird's life (which could be forty years, with good care). Is the tray an odd shape or size? Will paper need to be cut into unusual shapes to fit in it, or will paper towels, newspapers or clean sheets of used computer paper fit easily? The easier the tray is to remove and reline, the more likely you will be to change the lining of the tray daily. Can the cage tray be replaced if it becomes damaged and unusable?

You may notice that some of the cages for conures feature cage aprons, which help keep the debris your bird will create in the course of a day off your floor and somewhat under control. Cage aprons make cleaning up after your bird quicker and easier, and they also protect your carpet or flooring from discarded food and bird droppings if your bird decides to perch on the edge of her cage.

Finally, check the floor of the cage you've chosen. Does it have a grille that will keep your bird out of the debris that falls to the bottom of the cage, such as feces, seed hulls, molted feathers, and discarded food? To ensure your pet's long-term good health and to protect your conure from her own curious

Choose a cage with some horizontal bars so your bird can climb and space to hang up a variety of toys and perches.

nature, it's essential to have a grille between your pet and the debris in the cage tray. Also, it's easier to keep your conure in her cage while you're cleaning the cage tray if there's a grille between the cage and the tray.

The Cage Cover

One important, but sometimes overlooked, accessory is the cage cover. Be sure you have something to cover your conure's cage with when it's time to put your bird to sleep each night. The act of covering the cage seems to calm many pet

Setting Up the Cage

Make sure you have the cage all set up and ready before you bring your bird home, to help ease the transition for your pet. Here's how to set up your conure's cage.

- **Select the right location.** Your conure will be more comfortable if her cage is set up in a part of the house that you and your family use regularly, such as a family room. Your conure's cage should be out of the main traffic flow of the room, but still be in the room so you can include your bird in normal activities, such as watching TV. (Don't put your bird's cage near the kitchen or the bathroom, because cooking and chemical fumes from these rooms can harm your conure.)
- **Set the cage up with a solid wall behind it.** Your conure will feel more secure if she has a solid wall behind her cage because nothing can sneak up on her from behind.
- **Stagger the perches within the cage.** Don't place the perches at all the same height in the cage because your conure will be happier if she can perch at different heights at different times of the day.
- **Arrange the perches correctly.** Don't place perches directly over food or water bowls because pet birds eliminate regularly during the day, and you don't want your pet's food or water contaminated by her droppings.
- **Add some toys.** Your conure will need toys in her cage to help entertain her during the day. You should rotate the toys regularly to ensure your bird doesn't become bored with the same toys. You'll also have to replace those that your pet destroys during playtime. Don't overfill the cage with toys because your bird still needs room to move around. She needs to climb around in the cage and maybe even take short flights from end to end for exercise. She also needs to be able to get to the food and water bowls without interference from her toys.
- **Provide a cage cover.** Your conure will benefit from having her cage covered when she goes to sleep at night. Covering the cage will help your bird settle down at bedtime, which helps her establish a good daily routine.

birds and convince them that it's really time to go to bed, despite the sounds of an active family evening in the background.

You can purchase a cage cover or you can use an old sheet, blanket, or towel that is clean and free of holes. Be aware that some birds like to chew on their cage covers through the cage bars. If your bird does this, replace the cover when it becomes too tattered to do its job effectively. Replacing a well-chewed cover will also help keep your bird from becoming entangled in the cover or caught in a ragged clump of threads. Some birds have injured themselves quite severely by being caught in a chewed cage cover, so help keep your pet safe from this hazard.

What to Put in the Cage Tray

It is recommended that you use clean black-and-white newsprint, paper towels, or clean sheets of used computer printer paper. Sand, ground corncobs, or walnut shells may be sold by your pet supply store but are not recommended as cage flooring materials because they tend to hide feces and discarded food quite well. This can cause a bird owner to forget to change the cage tray on the principle that if it doesn't look dirty, it must not be dirty. This line of thinking can set up a thriving, robust colony of bacteria in the bottom of your bird's cage, which can

Place the cage where your conure will feel safe and comfortable but will still have plenty of interaction with your family.

lead to a sick bird if you're not careful. Newsprint and other paper products don't hide the dirt; in fact, they seem to draw attention to it, which leads conscientious bird owners to keep their pets' homes scrupulously clean.

You may see sandpaper or "gravel paper" sold in some pet stores as a cage tray liner. This product is supposed to provide a bird with an opportunity to ingest grit, which is purported to aid indigestion by providing coarse grinding material that helps break up food in the bird's gizzard. However, many avian experts do not believe that a pet bird needs grit, and if a bird stands on rough sandpaper, it could cause foot problems. For your pet's health, please don't use these gravel-coated papers.

Where to Put the Cage

Now that you've picked the perfect cage for your conure, where will you put it? Your conure will be happiest when she can feel like she's part of the family, so the living room, family room, or dining room may be among the best places for your bird.

Avoid keeping your bird in the bathroom or kitchen, because sudden temperature fluctuations or fumes from cleaning products used in those rooms could harm your pet. Another spot to avoid is a busy hall or entryway, because the activity level in these spots may be too much for your pet.

If possible, set up the cage so that it is at your eye level, because it will make servicing the cage and visiting with your pet easier for you. It will also reduce the stress on your conure, because birds like to be up high for security. Also, they do not like to have people or things looming over them, so consider items such as ceiling fans, chandeliers, or swag lamps. If members of your family are particularly tall, they may want to sit next to the cage or crouch down slightly to talk to the conure.

Whatever room you select for your conure's cage, be sure to put her in a secure corner (with one solid wall behind the cage to ensure her sense of security) and near a window. Please don't put the cage in direct sun, though, because conures can quickly overheat.

More to Buy

Along with the perfect size cage in the ideal location in your home, your conure will need a few cage accessories. These include food and water dishes, perches, and a playgym.

Dishes

Conures seem to enjoy food crocks, which are open ceramic bowls that allow them to hop up on the edge of the bowl and pick and choose what they will during the day. Crocks are also heavy enough to prevent mischievous birds from upending their food bowl, which can leave the bird hungry and you with quite a mess to clean up. You may also want to consider buying a cage with locking bowl holders, because bowls that are locked in place (but are still easy to remove by you at mealtime) are less likely to be tipped over by your conure.

If your conure doesn't tip over her bowls, she may do well with a clean plastic tray from a frozen dinner or a metal pie plate. Be sure to buy dishes that are less than one inch deep to ensure that your bird has easy access to her food at all times.

When buying dishes for your conure, be sure to pick up several sets so that mealtime cleanups are quick and easy.

Perches

When choosing perches for your pet's cage, try to buy two different diameters or materials so your bird's feet won't get tired of standing on the same-size perch of the same material day after day.

Birds spend all day on their feet and appreciate a variety of surfaces to stand and climb on.

Think of how tired your feet would feel if you stood on your bare feet on a piece of wood all day, then imagine how it would feel to stand on that piece of wood barefoot every day for years. Sounds pretty uncomfortable, doesn't it? That's basically what your bird has to look forward to if you don't vary her perching choices.

The recommended diameter for conure perches is three-quarters of an inch, so try to buy one perch of that size and one that is slightly larger (one inch, for example) to give your pet a chance to stretch her foot muscles. Birds spend almost all of their lives standing, so keeping their feet healthy is important. Also, avian foot problems are much easier to prevent than they are to treat.

You'll probably notice a lot of different kinds of perches when you visit your pet supply store. Along with the traditional wooden dowels, bird owners can now buy perches made from manzanita branches, PVC tubes, rope perches, and terracotta or concrete grooming perches.

Manzanita offers birds varied diameters on the same perch, along with chewing possibilities, while PVC is almost indestructible. (Make sure any PVC perches you offer your bird have been scuffed slightly with sandpaper to improve traction.) Rope perches also offer varied

> **TIP**
>
> **No Sandpaper**
>
> To help your bird avoid foot problems, do not use sandpaper covers on her perches. These abrasive sleeves, touted as nail trimming devices, really do little to trim a parrot's nails because birds don't usually drag their nails along their perches. What the sandpaper perch covers are good at doing, however, is abrading the surface of your conure's feet, which can leave her vulnerable to infections and can make movement painful.

diameter and a softer perching surface than wood or plastic, and terra cotta and concrete provide slightly abrasive surfaces that birds can use to groom their beaks without severely damaging the skin on their feet in the process. However, some bird owners have reported that their pets have suffered foot abrasions with these perches; watch your pet carefully for signs of sore feet (an inability to perch or climb, favoring a foot, or raw, sore skin on the feet) if you choose to use these perches in your pet's cage. If your bird shows signs of lameness, remove the abrasive perches immediately and arrange for your avian veterinarian to examine her.

When placing perches in your bird's cage, try to vary the heights slightly so your bird has different levels in her cage. Don't place any perches over food or water dishes, because birds will contaminate food or water by eliminating in it. Finally, place one perch higher than the rest for a nighttime sleeping roost. Conures and other parrots like to sleep on the highest point they can find to perch, so please provide this security for your pet.

The Playgym

Although your conure will spend quite a bit of time in her cage, she will also need time out of her cage to exercise and to enjoy a change of scenery. A *playgym* can help keep your pet physically and mentally active.

If you visit a large pet supply store or bird specialty store, or if you look through the pages of any pet bird hobbyist magazine, you will see a variety of playgyms on display. You can choose a complicated gym with a series of ladders,

Feral Conures

In southern California, bird watchers may find themselves being entertained by a feral flock of conures (cherry-heads, mitreds, and nandays are the most commonly seen species), Amazon parrots, and other psittacines. Bird lovers from the Pacific Palisades to Pasadena have been delighted by the antics of these feral birds, who regularly perform gymnastic routines on power lines and raid nut trees. They stay in an area for a few days, then move over a few city blocks to start the routine over again. Another flock has been reported on Telegraph Hill in San Francisco, and other flocks of feral conures have been sighted in Texas, Florida, and other temperate climate zones.

swings, perches, and toys, or you can purchase a simple T-stand that has a place for food and water bowls and a screw or two from which you can hang toys. If you're really handy with tools, you can even construct a gym to your conure's specifications.

As with the cage, the location of your conure's playgym will be an important consideration. You will want to place the gym in a secure location in your home that is safe from other curious pets, ceiling fans, open windows, and other household hazards. (Chapter 5, "Everyday Care," contains more information about making your home safe for your conure.) You will also want the gym to be in a spot frequented by your family, so your bird will have company while she plays and supervision so she doesn't get into unsafe situations.

Choosing the Right Toys

Your new pet has an active, agile mind that needs regular stimulation and challenges. A bored bird is often a destructive, noisy bird—not an ideal pet. Toys for a conure can be as complex as you care to buy or as simple as an empty paper towel roll. When selecting toys for your bird, keep a few safety tips in mind.

Size

Is the toy the right size for your bird? Large toys can be intimidating to small birds, which makes the birds less likely to play with them. On the other end of the spectrum, larger birds can easily destroy toys designed for smaller birds, and they can sometimes injure themselves severely in the process. Select toys for your conure that are designed for small- to medium-size parrots to ensure they are the proper size for your conure.

Safety

Is the toy safe? Good choices include sturdy wooden toys (either undyed or painted with bird-safe vegetable dye or food coloring) strung on closed-link chains or vegetable-tanned leather thongs, and rope toys. If you buy rope toys for your conure, make sure her nails are trimmed regularly to prevent them from snagging in the rope, and discard the toy when it becomes frayed to prevent accidents.

Unsafe items to watch out for are brittle plastic toys that can easily be shattered into fragments by a conure's busy beak, lead-weighted toys that can be cracked open to expose the dangerous lead to curious birds, loose link chains that can catch toenails or beaks, ring toys that are too small to climb through safely, and jingle-type bells that can trap toes, tongues, and beaks.

Don't assume every toy in the store is safe for your conure. Check for loose or brittle parts or toys that can catch a beak or a nail.

Conure Favorites

Conures kept as single pets sometimes enjoy mirrored toys. Make sure any mirrored toy you select is unbreakable, because your conure's busy beak will give it quite a workout. If you notice that your conure is becoming fixated on the pretty bird in the mirror, you should remove the mirrored toy and replace it with another safe, nonmirrored plaything.

Some entertaining toys can be made at home. Give your bird an empty paper towel roll or toilet paper tube (from unscented paper only, please), string some Cheerios on a piece of vegetable-tanned leather, or offer your bird a dish of raw pasta pieces to destroy.

Introducing New Toys

Conures are naturally curious, so introducing new toys to them should be a great adventure. You can set new toys next to your conure's cage to gauge her reaction. If she seems to want to know what the new item is, you can probably put it in the cage almost immediately. If your conure seems a bit apprehensive about the new toy, leave it by the cage for a few days to allow your pet to adjust to the presence of her new plaything.

Household Hazards

One of the reasons you chose a conure is because she's such a curious, active bird. These inquisitive little pets seem to be able to get into just about anything, which means they can get themselves into potentially dangerous situations rather quickly. Because of this natural curiosity, conure owners must be extremely vigilant when their birds are out of their cage.

Part of this vigilance should include bird-proofing your home. Parrot-proofing your home is akin to baby-proofing it. Remember that some parrots are intellectually on a level similar to that of a toddler. You wouldn't let a toddler have free run of your house without taking precautions to safeguard the child from harm, and you should have the same concern for your conure.

Let's go room by room and look at some of the potentially dangerous situations you should be aware of.

Bathroom

This can be a conure paradise if the bird is allowed to spend time with you as you prepare for work or for an evening out, but it can also be quite harmful to your bird's health. An open toilet could lead to drowning, the bird could hurt

Safe and Unsafe Houseplants

Safe	Unsafe
African violet	Amaryllis
Aloe	Bird of paradise
Burro's tail	Calla lily
Christmas cactus	Daffodil
Coleus	Dieffenbachia
Edible fig	English ivy
Ferns (asparagus, Boston, bird's nest, maidenhair, ribbon, staghorn, squirrel's foot)	Foxglove
	Holly
	Juniper
Gardenia	Lily-of-the-valley
Grape ivy	Marijuana
Hen and chicks	Mistletoe
Hibiscus	Oleander
Jade plant	Philodendron
Kalanchoe	Rhododendron
Palms (butterfly, cane, golden feather, Madagascar, European fan, sentry, and pygmy date)	Rhubarb
	Sweet pea
	Wisteria
Pepperomia	
Rubber plant	
Spider plant	
Yucca	

herself chewing on the electric cord of your blow-dryer, or she could be over-come by fumes from perfume, hairspray, or cleaning products, such as bleach, air freshener, and toilet bowl cleaner.

The bird could also become ill if she nibbles on prescription or nonprescription drugs in the medicine chest or she could injure himself by flying into a mirror. Use caution when taking your bird into the bathroom, and make sure her wings are clipped to avoid flying accidents.

Kitchen

This is another popular spot for birds and their owners to hang out, especially around mealtimes. Here again, dangers lurk for curious conures. An unsupervised

Make sure the plants in your home are safe for your conure.

bird could fly or fall into the trash can, or she could climb into the oven, dishwasher, freezer, or refrigerator and be forgotten. Your bird could land on a hot stove, or fall into an uncovered pot of boiling water or sizzling frying pan on the stove. The bird could also become poisoned by eating foods that are unsafe for her, such as chocolate, avocado, and rhubarb, if they are left unattended on a countertop.

Living Room

Are you sitting on your couch or in a comfortable chair as you read this book? Although it probably seems safe enough to you, your pet could be injured or killed if she decided to play hide-and-seek under pillows or cushions and you accidentally sat on her. Your conure could become poisoned by nibbling on a leaded glass lampshade, or she could fly out an open window or patio door. She could also fly into a closed window or door and injure herself severely. She could become entangled in a drapery cord or a Venetian blind pull, she could fall into an uncovered fish tank and drown, or she could ingest poison by nibbling on ashes or cigarette butts in an ashtray.

Home Office

This can be another conure playground, but you'll have to be on your toes to keep your pet from harming herself by nibbling on potentially poisonous markers, glue sticks or crayons, and electrical cords, or impaling herself on push pins.

Other Areas of Concern

If you have a ceiling fan in your house, make sure it is turned off when your bird is out of her cage. Make sure you know where your bird is before turning on your washer or dryer, and don't close your basement freezer without checking first to be sure your bird isn't in there. Lit candles, inlaid jewelry, sliding glass doors, and toxic houseplants also pose threats to your conure.

This doesn't mean you should keep your bird locked up in her cage all the time. On the contrary, all parrots need time out of their cage to maintain physical and mental health. The key is to be aware of some of the dangers that may exist in your home and to pay attention to your bird's behavior so you can intervene before the bird becomes ill or injured.

Nasty Fumes

Unfortunately, potential dangers to a pet bird don't stop with the furniture and accessories. A variety of fumes can overpower your conure, such as those from cigarettes, air fresheners, insecticides, bleach, shoe polish, oven cleaners, kerosene, lighter fluid, glues, active self-cleaning ovens, hairspray, overheated nonstick cookware, paint thinner, bathroom cleaners, and nail polish remover. Try to keep your pet away from anything that has a strong chemical odor, and be sure to apply makeup and hair care products far away from your conure.

To help protect your pet from harmful chemical fumes, consider using some "green" cleaning alternatives, such as baking soda and vinegar to clear clogged drains, baking soda instead of scouring powder to clean tubs and sinks, lemon juice and mineral oil to polish furniture, and white vinegar and water as a window cleaner. These products keep the environment a little friendlier for your bird, and these simple solutions to cleaning problems often work better than higher-priced, name-brand products.

Nonstick Cookware

Marathon cooking sessions may result in overheated cookware or stovetop drip pans, which could kill your bird if the cookware or drip pans are coated with a nonstick finish. As it burns, toxic fumes are released that can kill a beloved pet bird. You may want to consider replacing your nonstick cookware with stainless steel pots and pans, which you can treat with a nonstick cooking spray to make cleanups safe and easy. By the same token, the self-cleaning cycle on some ovens can create harmful fumes for pet birds. Use this cycle only if you have opened the windows around your bird's cage to let in fresh air. (Make sure your conure's cage is closed securely before opening a window.)

Home Improvements

If you're considering a remodeling or home improvement project, think about your conure first. Fumes from paint or formaldehyde, which can be found in carpet backing, paneling, and particleboard, can cause pets and people to become ill. If you are having work done on your home, consider boarding your conure at your avian veterinarian's office or at the home of a bird-loving friend or relative until the project is complete and the house is aired out. You can consider the house safe for your pet when you cannot smell any trace of any of the products used in the remodeling.

Pest Control

Having your home fumigated for termites poses another potentially hazardous situation for your pet conure. Ask your exterminator for information about the types of chemicals that will be used in your home, and inquire whether pet-safe formulas, such as electrical currents or liquid nitrogen, are available. If your house must be treated chemically, arrange to board your bird at your avian veterinarian's office or with a friend before, during, and after the fumigation to ensure that no harm comes to your bird. Make sure your house is aired out completely before bringing your bird home, too.

If you have other pets in the home who require flea treatments, consider using pyrethrin-based products in your home. These natural flea killers are derived from chrysanthemums and, although they aren't as long-lasting as synthetic substitutes, they do knock down fleas quickly and are safer in the long run for your pets and you. Or you can treat your dog's or cat's sleeping area with diatomaceous earth, which is the crushed shells of primitive one-celled algae. This dust kills fleas by mechanical means, which means that fleas will never develop a resistance to it as they could with chemical products.

Other Pets

Other pets can be harmful to your conure's health, too. A curious cat could claw or bite your bird, a dog could step on her accidentally or bite her, or another, larger bird could break her leg or rip off her upper mandible with her beak. If your conure tangles with another pet in your home, contact your avian veterinarian immediately because emergency treatment (for bacterial infection from a puncture wound or shock from being stepped on or suffering a broken bone) may be required to save your conure's life.

Chapter 5

Everyday Care

A conure requires care every day to ensure his health and well-being. Birds are happiest when they are secure and comfortable in a safe environment. You can help your conure feel more secure by establishing a daily routine and performing the same tasks at around the same time every day. This way, your conure knows his needs will be met by the people he considers to be his family.

Here are some of the things you'll need to do every single day for your conure:

- Observe your bird for any changes in his behavior or routine. Report any changes to your avian veterinarian immediately.
- Offer fresh food and remove old food. Wash the food dish thoroughly with detergent and water. Rinse thoroughly and allow the dish to air dry.
- Remove the water dish and replace it with a clean dish full of fresh water. Wash the soiled dish thoroughly with detergent and water.
- Change the paper in the cage tray.
- Let the bird out of his cage for supervised playtime.

Finally, you'll need to cover your bird's cage at about the same time every night to let him know it's bedtime. When you cover the cage, you'll probably hear your bird rustling around for a bit, perhaps getting a drink of water or a last mouthful of seeds before settling in for the night. Keep in mind that your conure will require ten to twelve hours of sleep a day, but you can expect that he will take naps during the day to supplement his nightly snooze.

Be Alert to Health Problems

Although it may seem a bit unpleasant to discuss, your bird's droppings require daily monitoring because they can tell you a lot about his general health. Conures will produce tubular droppings that appear green in the center with a whitish edge. These droppings are usually composed of equal amounts of fecal material (the green edge), urine (the clear liquid portion), and urates (the white or cream-colored center). A healthy conure generally eliminates between twenty-five and fifty times a day, although your bird may go more or less often.

Texture and consistency, along with frequency or lack of droppings, can let you know how your pet is feeling. For instance, if a bird eats a lot of fruits and vegetables, his droppings are generally looser and more watery than a bird who primarily eats seeds. But watery droppings can also indicate illness, such as diabetes or kidney problems, which causes a bird to drink more water than usual.

The color of the droppings can also be an indication of health. Birds who have psittacosis typically have bright lime-green droppings, while healthy birds have avocado or darker green and white droppings. Birds with liver problems may produce droppings that are yellowish or reddish, while birds who have internal bleeding will produce dark, tarry droppings.

Watch for changes in your bird's behavior or habits that could signal a problem.

TIP

Check the Dishes

Your bird should have clean water at all times, and this may mean refilling the water dish several times a day. Be sure to check your bird's seed dish daily, as well, to make sure he has seeds, rather than just empty seed hulls, in the dish. Refill the dish when necessary.

A color change doesn't necessarily indicate poor health. For example, birds who eat pelleted diets tend to have darker droppings than their seed-eating companions, and parrots who have gorged on a particular fresh food soon have droppings with that characteristic color. Birds who overindulge on beets, for instance, produce bright red droppings that can look as though the bird has suffered some serious internal injury. Birds who overdo it on sweet potatoes, blueberries, or raspberries produce orange, blue, or red droppings. During pomegranate season, birds who enjoy this fruit develop violet droppings that can look alarming to an unprepared owner.

As part of your daily cage cleaning and observation of your feathered friend, look at his droppings carefully. Learn what is normal for your bird in terms of color, consistency, and frequency and report any changes to your avian veterinarian promptly.

The holidays bring their own set of hazards for your bird. Be especially careful that decorations around your home are safe for your conure.

Seasonal Needs

Warm weather requires a little extra vigilance on your part to make sure your conure remains comfortable. To help keep your pet cool, keep him out of direct sun, offer him lots of fresh, juicy vegetables and fruits (be sure to remove these fresh foods from the cage promptly to keep your bird from eating spoiled food), and mist him lightly with a clean spray bottle filled with plain water. Use this bottle only for misting your bird.

On a warm day, you may notice your bird sitting with his wings held away from his body, rolling his

Cleaning the Cage

Cage cleaning should be part of your weekly care routine. Here's how to do it.

Remove your bird and all cage accessories before cleaning the cage.

Wipe off (or scrape off) old food from the cage bars and the corners of the cage.

Place the empty cage in the shower stall and turn on the shower. Running hot water over the cage helps loosen stuck-on food and other debris. Scrub the cage with a toothbrush or other stiff-bristled small brush to loosen anything that remains on the cage after it's been in the shower.

After all the debris has been removed, disinfect the cage with a bird-safe spray-on disinfectant that you can buy at a pet supply store. Let the disinfectant remain on the cage bars as directed by the instructions on the bottle and then rinse thoroughly to remove the disinfectant from the cage.

Dry the cage completely. While the cage is drying, clean the perches and accessories.

Scrape and wash the perches to keep them clean and free of debris. (Sand the perches with coarse grain sandpaper from time to time to improve traction for your pet.) Replace perches that are very chewed or cannot be cleaned.

Rotate the toys in the cage to keep your conure's environment interesting. Discard toys that are broken, frayed, or worn to protect your bird's health.

When the cage is completely dry, replace the accessories and put your bird back into his newly cleaned home.

Clean the playgym the same way you cleaned the cage.

tongue, and holding his mouth open. This is how a bird cools himself off. Watch your bird carefully on warm days because he can overheat quickly and may suffer heatstroke, which requires veterinary care. If you live in a warm climate, ask your avian veterinarian how you can protect your bird from this potentially serious problem.

Warm weather may also bring out a host of insect pests to bedevil you and your bird. Depending on where you live, you may see ants, mosquitoes, or other bugs around your bird's cage as the temperature rises. Take care to keep your

Holiday Precautions

The holidays bring their own special set of stresses, and they can also be hazardous to your conure's health. Drafts from frequently opening and closing doors can affect your bird's health, and the bustle of a steady stream of visitors can add to your pet's stress level (as well as your own).

Chewing on holiday plants, such as poinsettia, holly, and mistletoe, can make your bird sick, as can chewing on tinsel and ornaments. Round jingle-type bells can sometimes trap a curious bird's toe, beak, or tongue, so keep these holiday decorations out of your bird's reach. Watch your pet around strings of lights, too, as both the bulbs and the cords can be great temptations to curious beaks.

bird's cage scrupulously clean to discourage any pests, and remove any fresh foods promptly to keep insects out of your bird's food bowl. Finally, in cases of severe infestation, you may have to use Camicide or other bird-safe insecticides to reduce the insect population. (Remove your bird from the area of infestation before spraying.) If the problem becomes severe enough to require professional exterminators, make arrangements to have your bird stay out of the house for at least twenty-four hours after spraying has taken place.

You must also pay attention to your conure's needs when the weather turns cooler. You may want to use a heavier cage cover, especially if you lower the heat in your home at night, or move the bird's cage to another location in your home that is warmer and/or less drafty.

TIP

Background Noise

When you're away from home, leave a radio on for your bird. It provides background noise that keeps your pet's environment from becoming too quiet, which can be stressful for some birds.

Entertaining Your Conure

In addition to keeping your conure fed and clean, you must also look after his intellectual and emotional well-being. This means paying attention to your conure each and every day, and giving him things to do to challenge his mental and physical abilities.

Following is a list of games that will be as amusing for you as they are for your bird. As additional entertainment, offer your conure an interesting variety of food, both in the morning and in the evening. Make your pet work for some of his food to make meal-times mentally stimulating. Offer peas in the pod, peanuts or other nuts in the shell, or whole green beans.

- **The shell game:** This variation on the old carnival sideshow game is fun for your bird. In the avian version, you can hide a favorite treat under a nut cup or paper muffin cup and let your bird guess which shell hides the prize.
- **The great escape:** Offer your bird a clean, knotted-up piece of rope or vegetable-tanned leather and see how long it takes him to untie the knots. Give your bird extra points if he doesn't chew through any of the knots to untie them.

In addition to playing games with your bird, give him things he can use to amuse himself.

- **The mechanic:** Give your conure a clean nut and bolt with the nut screwed on and see how long it takes him to undo the nut. Make sure the nut and bolt are large enough that your pet won't accidentally swallow either while playing.

Good Intentions Gone Wrong

Bird owners and other people can unintentionally be a conure's worst enemy. At *Bird Talk*, we frequently heard from distraught owners who accidentally rolled over on their pets while bird and owner took a nap together, because the owner thought it would be cute to have the bird sleep with them.

Other owners would call, wanting someone to listen to their confession of accidentally stepping on a treasured pet or closing her in the refrigerator, freezer, washer, or dryer. Fortunately, in the case of the appliances, the bird's disappearance was usually noticed before any damage was done.

- **Peek-a-boo:** Put a beach towel loosely over your conure then let the bird work his way out from under it. Heap lavish amounts of praise on your pet for being so clever to find his way out.
- **Tug-of-war:** Give your bird one end of an empty paper towel roll and tug gently. Chances are your parrot won't easily let go, or if he does, he will quickly be back for more!

In addition to playing games, you should encourage your conure to learn how to entertain himself from an early age so he does not become overly dependent on you, because this overdependence may lead to screaming, feather picking, or other behavioral problems if the bird feels neglected.

Chapter 6

Feeding Your Conure

Conures can live to be 40 years old, but many pet birds do not live past age 15. In the past, when most pet conures were caught in the wild and imported, they rarely survived past the age of 10 due to their inadequate diet. Besides shortening a bird's life span, a poor diet causes a number of health problems, including respiratory infections, poor feather condition, flaky skin, and reproductive problems.

The good news for conure owners is that these birds are not known to be particularly fussy when it comes to food. They eat a wide variety of things and are not as shy about trying new foods as other parrot species may be.

A Balanced Diet

According to avian veterinarian Gary Gallerstein, birds require vitamins A, D, E, K, B1, B2, niacin, B6, B12, pantothenic acid, biotin, folic acid, and choline to stay healthy, but they can only partially manufacture vitamin D3 and niacin in their bodies. A balanced diet can help provide the rest.

Pet birds also need trace amounts of some minerals to maintain good health. These minerals are calcium, phosphorus, sodium, chlorine, potassium, magnesium, iron, zinc, copper, sulphur, iodine, and manganese. They can be provided with a well-balanced diet and a supplemental mineral block or cuttlebone.

Ideally, your conure's diet should contain about equal parts of seeds, grains, and legumes, and dark green or dark orange vegetables and fruits. You can supplement these with small amounts of well-cooked meat or eggs or dairy products. Let's look at each part of this diet in a little more detail.

Seeds, Grains, and Legumes

This portion of your bird's diet can include clean, fresh seed from your local pet supply store. Try to buy your birdseed from a store where stock turns over quickly. The dusty box on the bottom shelf isn't as nutritious for your pet as a bulk purchase of seeds from a freshly filled bin. When you bring the seeds home, refrigerate them to keep them from becoming infested with bugs.

To ensure your bird is receiving the proper nutrients from her diet, you need to know whether the seed you're serving is fresh. One way to do this is to try sprouting some of the seeds. Sprouted seeds can also tempt a finicky eater to broaden her diet.

To sprout seeds, you will need to soak them overnight in lukewarm water. Drain the water off and let the seeds sit in a closed cupboard or other out-of-the-way place for twenty-four hours. Rinse the sprouted seeds thoroughly before

Peanuts are interesting to eat as well as healthy. But never feed your bird salted nuts.

Fresh Sprouts

Serving sprouts is a simple and nutritious way to expand your conure's diet. Sprouted seed are packed with vitamins and are a tasty addition to her diet. All you need is a sprouting jar, some mesh cloth and a variety of seeds such as sunflower, mung, and radish. A health food store should carry this equipment, as well as instructions for sprouting seeds.

The first step is to wash and soak the seeds. The seeds should then be kept in a warm location to encourage sprouting. It is important that all of the material used is washed well to avoid spoiling. It takes about two to three days for the seeds to sprout, Once they have sprouted, offer them to your conure for a nutritious treat. Refrigerate the leftovers and don't keep them for more than a day or two.

---

offering them to your bird. If the seeds don't sprout, they aren't fresh and you'll need to find another source for your bird's food.

Be sure, too, that your pet has an adequate supply of seeds in her dish at all times. Some conures drop the empty seed hulls back into their dishes. This seemingly full dish can lead to a very hungry conure if you aren't observant enough to check the dish carefully. Rather than just looking in the dish while it's in the cage, I suggest that you take the dish out and inspect it over the trash can so you can empty the seed hulls and refill the dish easily.

Other items in the bread group that you can offer your pet include unsweetened breakfast cereals, whole-wheat bread, cooked beans, cooked rice and pasta. Offer a few flakes of cereal at a time, serve small bread cubes, and conure-size portions of rice, beans, or pasta.

One foodstuff that is quite popular with many conures is mung beans. Ask for them at your pet supply store and, if you're unsuccessful, check with a health food store or an Asian grocery in your area.

Fruits and Vegetables

Dark green or dark orange vegetables and fruits contain vitamin A, an important part of a bird's diet that is missing from seeds, grains, and legumes. This

Fresh fruit is an important part of your conure's diet.

vitamin helps fight off infection and keeps a bird's eyes, mouth, and respiratory system healthy. Some vitamin A-rich foods are carrots, yams, sweet potatoes, broccoli, dried red peppers, and dandelion greens.

You may be wondering whether to offer frozen or canned vegetables and fruits to your bird. Some birds will eat them, while others turn their beaks up at the somewhat mushy texture of these defrosted foodstuffs. The high sodium content in some canned foods may make them unhealthy for your conure. Frozen and canned foods will do in an emergency, but I would offer only fresh foods as a regular part of her diet.

Protein

Along with small portions of well-cooked meat, you can also offer your bird bits of tofu, water-packed tuna, fully cooked scrambled eggs, cottage cheese, unsweetened yogurt, or low-fat cheese. Don't overdo the dairy products, though, because a bird's digestive system lacks the enzyme lactase, which means she is unable to fully process dairy foods.

Introduce young conures to healthy people food early so that they learn to appreciate a varied diet. Some adult birds cling tenaciously to seed-only diets, which aren't healthy for them. Offer adult birds fresh foods, too, in the hope that they may try something new.

Whatever fresh foods you offer your pet, be sure to remove food from the cage promptly to prevent spoiling and to help keep your bird healthy. Ideally, you should change the food in your bird's cage every two to four hours (about every thirty minutes in warm weather), so a conure should be all right with a tray of food to pick through in the morning, another to select from during the afternoon, and a third fresh salad to nibble on for dinner.

Supplements

You may be concerned about whether your bird is receiving enough vitamins and minerals in her diet. If your conure's diet is mostly seeds and fresh foods, you may want to sprinkle a good-quality vitamin and mineral powder onto the fresh foods, where it has the best chance of sticking to the food and being eaten.

Vitamin-enriched seed diets may provide some supplementation, but some of them add the vitamins and minerals to the seed hulls, which your pet will discard while she's eating. Don't add vitamin and mineral supplements to your bird's water dish, because they can act as a growth medium for bacteria. They may also cause the water to taste different, which might discourage your bird from drinking.

What About Grit?

As a new bird owner, you may hear a lot of talk about the importance of grit in your bird's diet. Birds use grit in their gizzard to grind their food, much as we use our teeth. Avian veterinarians and bird breeders do not agree on how much grit birds need and how often it should be offered to them. Some will tell you birds need grit regularly while others will advise against it.

If your conure's breeder and your avian veterinarian think your bird needs grit, offer it sparingly (only about a pinch every few weeks). Do not offer it daily and do not provide your conure with a separate dish of grit because some birds will overeat the grit and suffer dangerous crop impactions as a result.

Water

You will need to provide your conure with fresh, clean water twice a day to maintain her good health. You may want to give your bird water in a shallow dish, or you may find that a water bottle does the trick. If you are considering a water bottle, be aware that some clever conures have been known to stuff a seed into the drinking tube, which lets all the water drain out of the bottle. This creates a thirsty bird and a soggy cage, neither of which are ideal.

Off Limits

Now that we've looked at foods that are good for your bird, let's look briefly at those that aren't. Among those foods considered harmful to pet birds are alcohol, rhubarb, avocado (the skin and the area around the pit can be toxic), as well as highly salted, sweetened, and fatty foods. You also want to avoid giving your bird seeds or pits from apples, apricots, cherries, peaches, pears, and plums, because they can be harmful.

Chocolate can kill your conure, so resist the temptation to share this snack with her. It contains the chemical theobromine, which birds cannot digest as completely as people can.

> **CAUTION**
>
> **Diet Taboos**
>
> Here's a little list to help you remember what foods to avoid:
>
> Alcohol
>
> Avocado
>
> Candy
>
> Chocolate
>
> Potato chips
>
> Pretzels
>
> Rhubarb
>
> Seeds or pits from apples, apricots, cherries, peaches, pears, and plums

Let common sense be your guide in choosing which foods can be offered to your bird: If it's healthy for you, it's probably okay to share. However, remember to reduce the size of the portion.

While sharing healthy people food with your bird is completely acceptable, sharing something that you've already taken a bite of is not. Human saliva has bacteria in it that are perfectly normal for people but that are potentially toxic to birds, so please don't share partially eaten food with your pet. For your bird's health and your peace of mind, give her a portion of her own, on her own plate.

The Pelleted Diet Option

Pelleted diets are created by mixing as many as forty different nutrients into a mash and then forcing the hot mixture through a machine to form various shapes. Some pelleted diets have colors and flavors added, while others are fairly plain.

These formulated diets provide balanced nutrition for your pet bird in an easy-to-serve form that reduces the amount of wasted food and eliminates the chance for a bird to pick through a smorgasbord of healthy foods to find her favorites and reject the foods she isn't particularly fond of. Some conures accept pelleted diets quickly, while others require some persuading.

To convert your pet to a pelleted diet, offer pellets alongside of or mixed in with her current diet. Once you see that your bird is eating the pellets, begin to gradually increase the amount of pellets you offer at mealtime while decreasing the amount of other food you serve. Within a couple of weeks, your bird should be eating her pellets with gusto!

Although most conures aren't shy about trying new foods, yours may be hesitant to accept pellets. If your conure seems a bit finicky about trying pellets, another bird in the house may show your conure how yummy pellets can be, or you

The advantage to a pelleted diet is that your bird can't just pick out her favorite foods and leave the rest untouched.

may have to act as if you are enjoying the pellets as a snack in front of your pet. Really play up your apparent enjoyment of this new food because it will pique your bird's curiosity and make the pellets seem exceedingly interesting.

Whatever you do, don't starve your bird into trying a new food. Offer new foods along with familiar favorites. This will ensure that your bird is eating and will also encourage her to try new foods. Don't be discouraged if your conure doesn't dive right in to a new food. Be patient, keep offering new foods to your bird, and praise her enthusiastically when she samples something new!

Chapter 7

Grooming Your Conure

Although birds preen and maintain their feathers on their own, your conure needs your help with several grooming chores. First, he should be able to bathe regularly, and you need to arrange his bath for him. He will also need to have his nails and flight feathers trimmed periodically to ensure his safety.

Although you might think your conure's beak also needs trimming, the fact is that a healthy bird supplied with enough chew toys seems to do a remarkable job of keeping his beak trimmed. If your bird's beak becomes overgrown, please consult your avian veterinarian. A parrot's beak contains a surprising number of blood vessels, so beak trimming is best left to the experts. Also, a suddenly overgrown beak may indicate that your bird is suffering from liver damage, a virus, or scaly mites, all of which require veterinary care.

Conures Love Water

As a general rule, conures are true water babies and can't get enough of being wet! If they can't bathe in their water bowl, a special bathing dish, or under the faucet in the kitchen or bathroom sink, they may take a quick roll through their food bowl, especially if there are a lot of damp, dark green, leafy vegetables in it. You may notice that your bird is particularly motivated to bathe when you vacuum the room in which he lives. Experts think the sound of a vacuum cleaner reminds conures of some distant time when they lived in the jungles and thunderstorms were brewing.

Regardless of how you provide the bird bath, be sure to set bath time early enough in the day so your pet's feathers can dry before bedtime, or you can use a blow dryer set on low to help the process along.

Unless your conure has gotten himself into oil, paint, wax, or some other substance that elbow grease alone won't remove and that could harm his feathers, he will not require soap as part of his bath. Under routine conditions, soaps and detergents can damage a bird's feathers by removing beneficial oils, so hold the shampoo during your conure's normal clean-up routine!

Nail Clipping

Conures need to have their nails clipped occasionally to prevent the nails from catching on toys or perches and injuring the bird. You need to remove only tiny portions of the nail to keep your conure's claws trimmed. Generally, a good guideline to follow is to only remove the hook on each nail, and to do this in the smallest increments possible.

Your conure's nails need regular care.

You may find that you have better luck filing your bird's nails with an emery board than with conventional nail clippers. Whatever method you choose, stop trimming well before you reach the quick (the bundle of nerves and blood vessels that runs through the center of the nail), which is difficult to see in a conure's black toenails. If you do happen to cut the nail short enough to make it bleed, apply cornstarch or flour, followed by direct pressure, to stop the bleeding.

Wing Trimming

The goal of a properly done wing trim is to prevent your bird from flying away or flying into a window, mirror, or wall while he's out of his cage. An added benefit of trimming your pet's wings is that his inability to fly well will make him more dependent on you for transportation, which should make him easier to handle. However, the bird still needs enough wing feathers so that he can glide safely to the ground if he is startled and takes flight from his cage top or playgym.

Because proper wing trimming is a delicate balance, you may want to enlist the help of your avian veterinarian, at least the first time. Wing trimming is a task that must be done carefully to avoid injuring your pet, so take your time if you're doing it yourself. Please do not just take up the largest pair of kitchen shears you own and start snipping away. I have heard stories from avian veterinarians about birds whose owners cut off their birds' wing tips (down to the bone) in this manner.

Be particularly alert after a molt, because your bird will have a whole new crop of flight feathers that need attention. You'll be able to tell when your bird is due for a trim when he starts becoming bolder in his flying attempts. Right after a wing trim, a conure generally tries to fly and finds he's unsuccessful at the attempt. He will keep trying, though, and may surprise you one day with a fairly good glide across his cage or off his playgym. If this happens, get the scissors and trim those wings immediately. If you don't, the section at the end of this chapter on finding lost birds may have more meaning for you.

C A U T I O N

Avoid Mite Protectors

Please don't buy mite protectors that hang on a bird's cage or conditioning products that are applied directly to a bird's feathers. Well-cared-for conures don't have mites and shouldn't be in danger of contracting them. (If your pet does have mites, veterinary care is the most effective treatment.) Also, the fumes from some of these products are quite strong and can be harmful to your pet's health.

Wing trimming is not as scary as it seems. The box on page 76 explains how to do it, step by step.

Tail Feathers

Under normal circumstances, your conure's tail feathers do not need trimming. Some conures may thrash their tail feathers in the course of their normal activities, and you may feel better about your bird's appearance if you trim the scruffy-looking feathers. However, if your bird's tail feathers are often damaged or ratty-looking, your conure's cage may be too small for him to move about easily and comfortably. Remember that your pet's cage should be spacious enough for him to move around easily, extend his wings fully, and not have the tip of his tail feathers touch the floor of the cage. If your bird's cage fails these simple tests, get a larger cage for your conure and use the smaller cage as a travel cage or as a temporary home when you're cleaning the main cage.

Wing Trimming Step by Step

The first step in trimming your conure's wing feathers is to assemble all the things you will need and find a quiet, well-lit place to groom your pet before you catch and trim him. I encourage you to groom your pet in a quiet, well-lit place because grooming excites some birds and causes them to become unsettled. Having good light to work under will make your job easier, and having a quiet work area may calm down your pet and make him a bit easier to handle.

Your grooming tools will include:

- Washcloth or small towel to wrap your conure in
- Small, sharp scissors to do the actual trimming
- Needle-nosed pliers (to pull out any blood feathers you may cut accidentally)
- Flour or cornstarch (not styptic powder) to stop the bleeding in case a blood feather is cut
- Nail trimmers (while you have your bird wrapped in the towel, you might as well do his nails, too)

Once you've assembled your supplies and found a quiet grooming location, drape the towel over your hand and catch your conure with your toweled hand. Gently grab your bird by the back of his head and neck (never compress the chest) and wrap him in the towel—firmly enough to hold him but not too tight! Hold your bird's head securely through the towel with your thumb and index finger. (Having the bird's head covered by the towel will calm him and will give him something to chew on while you clip his wings.)

Lay the bird on his back, being careful not to constrict or compress his chest (remember, birds have no diaphragms to help them breathe), and spread his wing out carefully. You will see an upper row of short feathers, called the *covert feathers*, and a lower row of long feathers, which are the *flight feathers*. Look for new flight feathers that are still growing in, also called blood feathers. These can be identified by their waxy, tight look (new feathers in their feather sheaths resemble the end of a shoelace) and their dark centers or quills—the dark color is caused by the blood supply to the new feather. **Never trim a blood feather.**

If your bird has a number of blood feathers, you may want to put off trimming his wings for a few days, because older, fully grown feathers act as a cushion to protect those just coming in from life's hard knocks. If your bird has only one or two blood feathers, you can trim the full-grown feathers accordingly.

To trim your bird's feathers, separate each one away from the other flight feathers and cut it individually (remember, the goal is to have a well-trimmed bird who is still able to glide a bit if he needs to). Start from the tip of the wing when you trim and clip just five to eight feathers in. Use the primary covert feathers (the set of feathers above the primary flight feathers) as a guideline as to how short you should trim—trim the flight feathers so they are just a tiny bit longer than the coverts.

Be sure to trim an equal number of feathers from each wing. Although some people think that a bird needs only one trimmed wing, this is incorrect and could actually harm a bird who tries to fly with one trimmed and one untrimmed wing. Think of how off balance that would make you feel; your conure is no different.

Now that you've successfully trimmed your bird's wing feathers, congratulate yourself. You've just taken a great step toward keeping your conure safe. Now you must remember to check your conure's wing feathers and retrim them periodically (about four times a year is a minimum).

Blood Feather First Aid

If you do happen to cut a blood feather, remain calm. You must remove it and stop the bleeding to ensure that your bird doesn't bleed to death, and panicking will do neither of you any good.

To remove a blood feather, take a pair of needle-nosed pliers and grasp the broken feather's shaft as close to the skin of the wing as you can. With one steady motion, pull the feather out completely. After you've removed the feather, put a pinch of flour or cornstarch on the feather follicle (the spot you pulled the feather out of) and apply direct pressure for a few minutes until the bleeding stops. If the bleeding doesn't stop after a few minutes of direct pressure, or if you can't remove the feather shaft, contact your avian veterinarian immediately for further instructions.

Although it may seem like you're hurting your conure by removing the broken blood feather, consider this: A broken blood feather is like an open faucet. If left in, the faucet stays open and lets the blood out. Once removed, the bird's skin generally closes up behind the feather shaft and shuts off the faucet.

Molting

At least once a year, your conure will lose his feathers. Don't be alarmed—this is a normal process called molting. Many pet birds seem to be in a perpetual molt, with feathers falling out and coming in throughout the summer.

> **TIP**
>
> **Comfort During Molting**
>
> Encourage balanced nutrition.
>
> Decrease stress by emphasizing security and rest periods.
>
> Keep the room temperature between 75° and 80° during heavy shedding.
>
> Promote preening activity.

You can consider your bird to be in molting season when you see many whole feathers in the bottom of the cage and you notice that he seems to have broken out in a rash of stubby little bumps that look like aglets (the plastic tips on the ends of your shoelaces). These bumps are the feather sheaths that help new pinfeathers break through the skin, and they are made of keratin (the same material that makes up your fingernails). The sheaths also help protect growing feathers from damage until the feather completes its growth cycle.

You may notice that your conure is a little more irritable during the molt; this is to be expected. Think about how you would feel if you suddenly had all these itchy new feathers coming in. However, your bird may actively seek out more time with you during the molt, because owners are handy to have around when a conure has an itch on the top of his head that he can't quite scratch!

Scratch these new feathers gently, because some of them may still be growing in and may be sensitive to the touch. You may want to try

A molting bird may look a bit unkempt and act a little irritable.

rolling the newly forming feathers gently between your fingers to open up the feather sheaths without causing your conure too much discomfort.

Some birds may benefit from special conditioning foods during the molt. Check with your avian veterinarian to see if your bird is a candidate for these foods.

If Your Conure Flies Away . . .

Now that we have covered wing trimming, it's as good a time as any to discuss the possibility of your bird escaping. One of the most common accidents that befalls bird owners is that a fully flighted bird (one with untrimmed wings) escapes through an open door or window. Just because your bird has never flown before or shown any interest in leaving his home—or even his cage—doesn't mean that he can't fly or that he won't become disoriented once he's outside. If you don't believe it can happen, just check the lost and found advertisements in your local newspaper for a week. Chances are many birds will turn up in the "lost" column, and few are ever found.

Why don't lost birds come home? Some fall victim to predators in the wild, while others join flocks of feral, or wild, parrots (Florida and California are particularly noted for these). Still other lost birds end up miles away from home because they fly wildly and frantically in any direction. And the people who find them don't advertise in the same area that the birds were lost in. Finally, some people who find lost birds don't advertise that they've been found because the finders think that whoever was unlucky or uncaring enough to lose the bird in the first place doesn't deserve to have him back.

Trimming your conure's flight wings will help keep him safe and at home.

Keeping Your Bird Safe

How can you prevent your bird from becoming lost? Here are some tips:

- Make sure his wings are safely trimmed at regular intervals.
- Trim both wings evenly and remember to trim them after your bird has molted.
- Make sure your bird's cage door locks securely and that his cage tray cannot come lose if the cage is knocked over or dropped accidentally.
- Check your window screens to be sure they fit securely and are free from tears and holes.
- Keep all window screens and patio doors closed when your bird is at liberty.
- Never go outside with your bird on your shoulder.

How to Catch an Escaped Bird

If, despite your best efforts, your bird escapes, you must act quickly for the best chance of recovering your pet. Here are some things to keep in mind:

- If possible, keep the bird in sight. This will make chasing him easier.
- Make an audiotape of your bird's voice (so you're ready for just such an emergency) and play it outside on a portable tape recorder to lure your bird back home.
- Place your bird's cage in an area where he is likely to see it, such as on a deck or a patio. Put lots of treats and food on the floor of the cage to tempt your pet back into his home.
- Use another caged bird to attract your conure's attention.
- Alert your avian veterinarian's office that your bird has escaped. Also let the local humane society and other veterinary offices in your area know.
- Post fliers in your neighborhood describing your bird. Offer a reward and include your phone number.
- Don't give up hope.

Chapter 8

Keeping Your Conure Healthy

In general, conures have a strong survival instinct, and even when ill, will continue to act normally for long periods of time. But conures, like all pets, can get sick or injured. Since birds can't describe how they are feeling, it is very important that you understand the basics of your pet's physiology as well as the signs of illness. With preventive measures, early detection, and good care, the odds for a successful recovery are great.

Avian Anatomy

You may be surprised to find out that your conure's body is not all that different from your own body. You both have skin, skeleton, respiratory, cardiovascular, digestive, excretory, and nervous systems, and sensory organs, although the various systems work in slightly different ways.

Skin

Your bird's skin is difficult to see, since your conure has so many feathers. If you part the feathers carefully, though, you can see thin, seemingly transparent skin and the muscles beneath it. Modified skin cells help make up your bird's beak, cere, claws, and the scales on her feet and legs.

Birds cannot perspire as mammals do because birds have no sweat glands, so they must have a way to cool themselves off. On a warm day, you may notice your bird sitting with her wings held away from her body, rolling her tongue, and holding her mouth open. This is how a bird cools herself off. Watch your bird carefully on warm days because she can overheat quickly, and she may suffer from heatstroke, which requires veterinary care. If you live in a warm climate, ask your avian veterinarian how you can protect your bird from this serious problem.

Musculoskeletal System

Next, let's look at your bird's skeleton. Did you know that some bird bones are hollow? These are lighter, making flying easier, but it also means these bones are more susceptible to breakage. For this reason, you must always handle your bird carefully! Another adaptation for flight is that the bones of a bird's wing (which correspond to our arm and hand bones) are fused for greater strength.

Birds also have air sacs in some of their bones (these are called pneumatic bones) and in certain body cavities that help lighten the bird's body and also cool her more efficiently.

Parrots have ten neck vertebrae, compared to a human's seven. This makes a parrot's neck more mobile than a person's (a parrot can turn her head almost 180 degrees). This gives the parrot an advantage in spotting food or predators in the wild.

A tiny conure has more vertebrae in her neck than you do, making it possible for her to look way over her shoulder.

During breeding season, a female bird's bones become denser to enable her to store the calcium needed to create eggshells. A female's skeleton can weigh up to 20 percent more during breeding season than she does the rest of the year because of this calcium storage.

Respiratory System

Your bird's respiratory system is highly efficient and works in a markedly different way from yours. Here's how your bird breathes: Air enters the body through your bird's nares and passes through her sinuses and into her throat. As it does, the air is filtered through the choana, which is a slit that can easily be seen in the roof of many birds' mouths. The choana also helps clean and warm the air before it goes further into the respiratory system.

After the air passes the choana, it flows through the larynx and trachea, past the syrinx or voice box. Your bird doesn't have vocal cords like you do; rather, vibrations of the syrinx membrane are what enable birds to make sounds.

So far it sounds similar to the way we breathe, doesn't it? Well, here's where the differences get bigger. As the air continues its journey past the syrinx and into the bronchi, your bird's lungs don't expand and contract to bring the air in and push it out. This is partly due to the fact that birds don't have diaphragms, as people do. Instead, the bird's body wall expands and contracts, much like a fireplace bellows. This action brings air into the air sacs mentioned earlier as part of the skeleton. This bellows action also moves air in and out of the lungs.

Although a bird's respiratory system is extremely efficient at exchanging gases in the system, two complete breaths are required to do the same work that a single breath does in people and other mammals. This is why you may notice that your bird seems to be breathing quite quickly.

Nervous System

Your conure's nervous system is very similar to your own. Both are made up of the brain, the spinal cord, and countless nerves throughout the body that transmit messages to and from the brain.

Cardiovascular System

Along with the respiratory system, your bird's cardiovascular system keeps oxygen and other nutrients moving throughout her body, although the circulatory path in your conure differs from yours. In your conure, blood flowing from the legs, reproductive system, and lower intestines passes through the kidneys on its way back to the general circulatory system.

Like you, though, your conure has a four-chambered heart, with two atria and two ventricles. Unlike your average heart rate of 72 beats per minute, your conure's average heart rate is 340 to 600 beats per minute.

Digestive System

Your bird's body needs fuel for energy. Birds' bodies are fueled by food, which is where your bird's digestive system comes in. The digestive system provides the fuel that maintains your bird's body temperature—which is higher than yours. (The first time I bird-sat for friends, I worried about their cockatoo's seemingly hot feet. After another bird owner told me that birds have higher temperatures than people, though, I stopped worrying about the bird's warm feet.)

Your conure's digestive system begins with her beak. The size and shape of a bird's beak depend on her food-gathering needs. Compare and contrast the sharp, pointed beak of an eagle or the elongated bill of a hummingbird with the hooked beak of your conure. Notice the underside of your bird's upper beak if you can. It has tiny ridges in it that help your conure hold and crack seeds more easily.

Parrots don't have saliva to break down and move their food, as we do. After the food leaves your bird's mouth, it travels down the esophagus, where it is moistened.

Birds need to eat frequently to maintain their high body temperature.

The food then travels to the crop, where it is moistened further and is passed in small increments into the bird's gizzard. Between the crop and the gizzard, food passes through the proventriculus, where digestive juices are added. Once in the gizzard, the food is broken down into even smaller pieces. The food next travels to the small intestine, where nutrients are absorbed into the bloodstream. Anything that's left over travels through the large intestine to the cloaca, which is the common chamber that collects wastes before they leave the bird's body through the vent.

Along with the solid waste created by the digestive system, your conure's kidneys create urine, which is transported through ureters to the cloaca for excretion. Unlike a mammal, a bird does not have a bladder or a urethra.

Feathers

Birds are the only animals that have feathers, and they serve several purposes. Feathers help birds fly, they keep birds warm, they attract the attention of potential mates, and they help scare away predators.

Did you know that your conure has between 2,000 and 3,000 feathers on her body? These feathers grow from follicles that are arranged in rows known as *pterylae*. The unfeathered patches of bare skin on your conure's body are called *apteria*.

A feather is a remarkably designed creation. The base of the feather shaft, which fits into the bird's skin, is called the *quill*. It is light and hollow, but remarkably tough. The upper part of the feather shaft is called the *rachis*. From the rachis branch the barbs and barbules (smaller barbs) that make up most of the feather. The barbs and barbules have small hooks on them that enable the different parts of the feather to interlock like Velcro and form the feather's vane or web.

Feather colors are determined by combinations of pigment in the outer layer and in the interior structure of the feather.

Birds have several different types of feathers on their bodies. Contour feathers are the colorful outer feathers on the body and wings. Many birds have an undercoating of down feathers that helps keep them warm. Semiplume feathers are found on a bird's beak, nares (nostrils), and eyelids.

A bird's flight feathers can be classified into one of two types. *Primary* flight feathers are the large wing feathers that push a bird forward during flight. They are also the ones that need clipping, which we discussed in chapter 7, "Grooming Your Conure." *Secondary* flight feathers are found on the inner wing, and they help support the bird in flight. Primary and secondary flight feathers can operate independently. The bird's tail feathers also assist in flight by acting as a brake and a rudder.

To keep their feathers in good condition, birds spend a lot of time fluffing and preening.

To keep their feathers in good condition, healthy birds spend a great deal of time fluffing and preening. You may see your conure seeming to pick at the base of her tail on the top side. This is a normal behavior in which the bird removes oil from the preen gland and spreads it on her feathers. The oil helps prevent skin infections and waterproofs the feathers.

Sometimes pet birds will develop white lines or small holes on the large feathers of their wings and tails. These lines or holes are referred to as stress bars or stress lines, and result from the bird being under stress as the feathers were developing. If you notice stress bars on your bird's feathers, discuss them with your avian veterinarian. Be prepared to describe anything new in your pet's routine to the veterinarian, because parrots are creatures of habit and sometimes react negatively to changes in their surroundings, diet, or daily activities.

Avian Senses

Taste

Compared to other mammals, the sense of taste is poorly developed in conures. Birds can taste, but in a limited way because they have fewer taste buds in their mouths than people do. Also, their taste buds are contained in the roofs of their mouths, (not in the tongue, as ours are). Experts therefore think a parrot's sense of taste is poorly developed.

Vision

Conures have a well-developed sense of sight. Birds see detail and they can discern colors. Be aware of this when selecting cage accessories for your pet, because some birds react to changes in the color of their food dishes. Some seem excited by a different color bowl, while others act fearful of the new item.

Because their eyes are located on the sides of their heads, most pet birds rely on monocular vision, which means they use each eye independent of the other. If a bird wants to study an object, you will see her tilt her head to one side and examine the object with just one eye.

Like cats and dogs, birds have a third eyelid called the nictitating membrane that you will sometimes see flick briefly across your conure's eye. The purpose of this membrane is to keep the eyeball moist and clean. If you see your conure's nictitating membrane for more than a brief second, contact your avian veterinarian for an evaluation.

You have probably noticed that your bird lacks eyelashes. In their place are small feathers called semiplumes that help keep dirt and dust out of the bird's eyeball.

Hearing

You may be wondering where your conure's ears are. Look carefully under the feathers behind and below each eye to find them. The ears are somewhat large holes in the sides of your bird's head. Conures have about the same ability to distinguish sound waves and determine the location of the sound as people do, but birds seem to be less sensitive to higher and lower pitches than their owners.

Smell

How does your conure's sense of smell compare to your own? Birds

Your conure's ears are behind and below each eye. You can see a very slight break in the feathers on this bird.

seem to have a poorly developed sense of smell because smells often dissipate quickly in the air (where flying birds spend the majority of their time).

Touch

The final sense we relate to, touch, is well-developed in parrots. Parrots use their feet and their mouths to touch their surroundings (young birds, particularly, seem to "mouth" everything they can get their beaks on), to play, and to determine what is safe to perch on or chew on or eat.

Along with their tactile uses, a parrot's feet also have an unusual design compared to other caged birds. Unlike a finch, for example, which has three toes pointing forward and one back, two of the conure's toes point forward and two point backward in an arrangement called *zygodactyl*. This enables a parrot to climb up, down, and around trees easily. Some larger parrots also use their feet to hold food or to play with toys.

Visiting the Veterinarian

With good care, a conure can live up to 40 years, although the average life span of a pet conure is about 15 years. One of the reasons conures don't live longer is that their owners may be reluctant to take their pets to the veterinarian. Some people don't want to pay veterinary bills for relatively "inexpensive" birds.

Choosing an Avian Veterinarian

As a caring owner, you want your bird to have good care and the best chance to live a long, healthy life. To that end, you will need to find a veterinarian who understands the special medical needs of birds and one with whom you can establish a good working relationship. The best time to do this is when you first bring your conure home from the breeder or the pet store. If possible, arrange to visit your veterinarian's office on your way home from the breeder or store. This is particularly important if you have other birds at home, because you don't want to endanger the health of your existing flock or your new pet.

If you don't know an avian veterinarian in your area, ask the person from whom you bought your conure where they take their birds. (Breeders and bird stores usually have avian veterinarians on whom they depend.) Talk to other bird owners you know and find out whom they take their pets to, or call bird clubs in your area for referrals.

If you have no bird-owning friends or can't locate a bird club, your next best bet is the Yellow Pages. Read the advertisements for veterinarians carefully and try to find one who specializes in birds. Many veterinarians who have an interest in treating birds will join the Association of Avian Veterinarians and advertise themselves as members of this organization. Some veterinarians have taken and passed a special examination that entitles them to call themselves avian specialists.

Once you've received your recommendations or found likely candidates in the telephone book, start calling the veterinary offices. Ask the receptionist how many birds the doctor sees in a week or month, how much an office visit costs, and what payment options are available (cash, credit card, check, or time payments). You can also inquire whether the doctor keeps birds as pets.

Alternative Health Treatments

Homeopathic treatments, herbal remedies, and acupuncture have become commonplace alternative medical treatments for people today, but did you know they can also be used to treat pet birds? Veterinarians began investigating alternative health treatments for pets in the 1980s, and today pet bird owners may be able to choose such treatments for their birds.

Birds may be good candidates for alternative medical treatments because of their physical and emotional makeup. Their natures are well-suited to a holistic approach, which takes into account the bird's whole environment and routine when evaluating her health or illness. A bird owner who practices a holistic approach to bird care will carefully evaluate their bird daily for signs of illness while feeding her a top-quality diet and ensuring that the bird has an interesting and varied routine each day. If something is out of the ordinary during the owner's daily evaluation, the owner contacts an avian veterinarian for an appointment as soon as the change is noted, rather than waiting to see what might happen to the bird.

Look in the Yellow Pages for veterinarians in your area who include holistic or alternative treatments in their practice and call the office to find out whether the doctor treats birds. If you don't have a holistic veterinarian in your area, discuss alternative treatment options with your avian veterinarian to see whether they are an option for your conure when she is ill or injured.

If you like the answers you receive from the receptionist, make an appointment for your conure to be evaluated. (If you don't, of course, move on to the next name on your list.) Make a list of any questions you want to ask the doctor regarding your bird's diet, how often your bird's wings and nails should be clipped, how often you should bring the bird in for an examination, and anything else you feel you need to know.

Birds are unique among companion animals, and that means you really need to see a veterinarian who specializes in treating them.

Plan to arrive a little early for your first appointment because you will be asked to fill out a patient information form. This form will ask you for your bird's name, her age and sex, the length of time you have owned her, your name, address and telephone number, your preferred method of paying for veterinary services, how you heard about the veterinary office, and the name and address of a friend the veterinary office can contact in case of emergency. The form may also ask you to express your opinion on the amount of money you would spend on your pet in an emergency, because this can help the doctor know what kind of treatment to recommend in such instances.

What the Veterinarian May Ask You

Do not be afraid to ask your avian veterinarians questions. Avian vets have devoted a lot of time, energy, and effort to studying birds, so put this resource to use whenever you can.

You may also be asked a number of questions by the veterinarian. These may include:

- Why is the bird here today?
- What is the bird's normal activity level?

- How is the bird's appetite?
- What does the bird's normal diet consist of?
- Have you noticed a change in the bird's appearance lately?

Be sure to explain any changes in as much detail as you can, because changes in your bird's normal behavior can indicate illness.

The Physical Exam

After the question-and-answer session with you, the exam will begin. Your veterinarian will probably take his or her first look at your conure while she is still in her cage or carrier. The veterinarian does this to give the bird a chance to become accustomed to her surroundings, rather than reaching in and grabbing your pet. While the veterinarian is talking to you, he or she will check the bird's feather condition, her overall appearance, posture, and perching ability.

Next, the doctor will drape a towel over his or her hand and gently catch your conure and remove her from her carrier or cage. When the bird is out of her carrier, the doctor will look her over carefully. He or she will note the condition of your pet's eyes, her beak, and her nares. He or she will weigh your bird in a device that looks like a metal colander balanced on a scale, and the doctor will feel, or palpate, your bird's body, wings, legs, and feet for any abnormalities. He or she will also examine the bird's feathers.

Health Insurance for Birds?

Did you know that pet birds can now qualify for health insurance? Health insurance has been available for pet dogs and cats since the early 1980s, and bird owners began to be able to take advantage of the benefits of pet health insurance in the late 1990s.

Pet bird health insurance coverage can cover major medical treatments and surgeries, laboratory fees, prescriptions, X-rays, and hospitalization. Birds may also be covered for self-mutilation and feather picking as well as routine care. Ask your avian veterinarian for more information about health insurance for your pet bird.

Common Avian Veterinary Tests

After your veterinarian has completed your conure's physical examination, he or she may recommend further tests. These can include:

- Blood workups help a doctor determine whether your bird has a specific disease. Blood tests can be further broken down into a complete blood count, which determines how many platelets, red and white blood cells your bird has (this information can help diagnose infections or anemia), and a blood chemistry profile, which helps a veterinarian analyze how your bird's body processes enzymes, electrolytes, and other chemicals.
- X-rays enable a veterinarian to study the size and shape of a bird's internal organs and the structure of her bones. X-rays also help doctors find foreign bodies in a bird's system.
- Microbiological exams help a veterinarian determine whether any unusual organisms (bacteria, fungi, or yeast) are growing inside your bird's body.
- Fecal analysis studies a small sample of your bird's droppings to determine whether she has internal parasites or a bacterial or yeast infection.

Follow-Up Health Care

Once the examination is concluded and you've had a chance to discuss any questions you have with your veterinarian, the doctor will probably recommend a follow-up examination schedule for your pet. Most healthy birds visit the veterinarian annually, but some need to go more frequently.

To help your veterinarian and to keep your pet from suffering long-term health risks, keep a close eye on her daily activities and appearance. If something suddenly changes in the way your bird looks or acts, contact your veterinarian immediately. Birds naturally hide signs of illness to protect them from predators, so by the time a bird looks or acts sick, she may already be dangerously ill.

Conure Health Concerns

Conures are prone to feather picking, papillomas, and psittacine beak and feather disease syndrome (PBFDS). Conures fed seed-only diets can also develop a vitamin A deficiency and other nutritional disorders.

When conures were being imported in large numbers, some of them developed a condition called *conure bleeding syndrome*, which I will discuss briefly in the following section, although it does not appear with the frequency it did at the height of importation.

Conure Bleeding Syndrome

Conure bleeding syndrome has been documented in blue-crowns, peach-fronts, half-moons, and Patagonians. Affected birds suffer episodes of internal bleeding that eventually kill them. These birds will have nosebleeds, difficulty breathing, weakness, diarrhea, and excessive urination. The cause is unknown, but a lack of vitamin K, calcium, and other minerals in a bird's diet may contribute to conure bleeding syndrome. Other veterinary experts believe the condition is caused by a virus.

Papillomas

Papillomas are benign tumors that can appear almost anywhere on a bird's skin, including her foot, leg, eyelid, or preen gland. These tumors, which are caused by a virus, can appear as small, crusty lesions, or they may be raised growths that have a bumpy texture or small projections. If a bird has a papilloma on her cloaca, the bird may appear to have a wet raspberry coming out of her vent.

Many papillomas can be left untreated without harm to the bird, but some must be removed by an avian veterinarian because a bird can pick at the growth and cause it to bleed.

Any sudden change in your bird's appearance could be a sign of trouble and needs to be checked out.

Signs of Illness

To help your veterinarian and to protect your pet from long-term health problems, keep a close eye on her daily activities and appearance. If something suddenly changes in the way your bird looks or acts, contact your veterinarian immediately. Birds naturally hide signs of illness to protect themselves from predators, so by the time a bird looks or acts sick, she may already be dangerously ill.

Some signs of illness include

- A fluffed-up appearance
- Loss of appetite
- Sleeping all the time
- A change in the appearance or number of droppings
- Weight loss
- Listlessness
- Drooping wings
- Lameness
- Partially eaten food stuck to the face or food has been regurgitated onto the cage floor
- Labored breathing, with or without tail bobbing
- Runny eyes or nose
- Stops whistling, talking, or singing

If your bird shows any of these signs, please contact your veterinarian's office immediately.

Psittacine Beak and Feather Disease Syndrome

PBFDS is a virus that has been reported in more than forty species of parrots, including conures. PBFDS causes a bird's feathers to become pinched or clubbed in appearance. Other symptoms include beak fractures and mouth ulcers. This highly contagious, fatal disease is most common in birds under three years of age, and there is no cure at present. A vaccine is under development at the University of Georgia.

Feather Picking

Conure owners, particularly those who own nandays and suns, need to be on the alert for feather picking. Don't confuse picking with normal preening. Birds who pick their feathers pluck them right out. You will see feathers on the floor of the cage and scruffy or even bald spots on your bird. Once feather picking begins, it may be difficult to get a bird to stop. Although it looks painful to us, some birds find the routine of pulling out their feathers emotionally soothing.

Conures who suddenly begin picking their feathers, especially those under the wings, may have an intestinal parasite called *giardia*. If you notice that your bird suddenly starts pulling her feathers out, contact your avian veterinarian for an evaluation. Other causes to consider include poor diet, low humidity, infrequent baths, and lack of access to regular periods of light.

A bored or stressed bird may mutilate her beautiful feathers.

Psychological causes for feather picking can include boredom, insecurity, breeding frustrations, nervousness, and stress. Stress in a bird's life can result from something as simple as rearranging the living room furniture or as complex as bringing a new child or pet into the home.

I don't have a magic solution to offer, except to ask that you have your bird evaluated by your avian veterinarian if she starts to pick. If the cause isn't physical, please be patient with your feather-picking parrot as you try to distract her away from her feathers.

Conure First Aid

Sometimes your pet will get herself into a situation that will require quick thinking and even quicker action on your part to help save her from serious injury or death. Here are some basic first-aid techniques that may prove useful in these situations. Before we get into the specific techniques, though, make sure you have your bird owner's first aid kit. (See "Your Conure's First Aid Kit" in the box on page 97 for information on what to include.)

Here are some urgent medical situations bird owners are likely to encounter, the reason they are medical emergencies, the signs and symptoms your bird might show, and what you should do for your bird.

What to Do in an Emergency

If your bird requires urgent care, keep the following in mind:

Stay as calm as possible.
Stop any bleeding.
Keep the bird warm.
Keep the bird calm and quiet.
Call your veterinarian's office for additional instructions.
Describe what has happened to your bird.
Listen carefully to any instructions you receive.
Take your bird to the veterinarian's office or veterinary
    urgent care clinic as soon as possible.

Animal Bites

It's an emergency because: Infections can develop from bacteria on the biting animal's teeth and/or claws. Also, a bird's internal organs can be damaged by the bite.

Signs: Sometimes the bite marks can be seen, but often the bird shows few, if any, signs of injury.

What to do: Call your veterinarian's office and transport the bird there immediately. Treatment for shock and antibiotics are often the steps veterinarians take to save birds who have been bitten.

Beak Injury

It's an emergency because: A bird needs both her upper and lower beak (also called the upper and lower mandible) to eat and preen properly. Infections can also set in rather quickly if a beak is fractured or punctured.

Signs: The bird is bleeding from her beak. This often occurs after the bird flies into a windowpane or a mirror, or if she has a run-in with a ceiling fan. The bird may also have cracked or damaged her beak, and portions of the beak may be missing.

What to do: Control the bleeding (see the following section), keep the bird calm and quiet, and contact your avian veterinarian's office.

Your Conure's First Aid Kit

Assemble a bird owner's first aid kit so that you will have some basic supplies on hand before your bird needs them. Here's what to include:

- Appropriate-size towels for catching and holding your bird
- Heating pad, heat lamp, or other heat source
- Pad of paper and pencil to make notes about the bird's condition
- Styptic powder, silver nitrate stick, or cornstarch to stop bleeding (use styptic powder or silver nitrate stick on beak and nails only)
- Blunt-tipped scissors
- Nail clippers and nail file
- Needle-nosed pliers to pull broken blood feathers
- Blunt-end tweezers
- Hydrogen peroxide or other disinfectant solution
- Eye irrigation solution
- Bandage materials such as gauze squares, masking tape (it doesn't stick to a bird's feathers as adhesive tape does), and gauze rolls
- Pedialyte or other energy supplement
- Eyedropper
- Small syringes without the needles to irrigate wounds or feed sick birds
- Penlight

Bleeding

It's an emergency because: A bird can withstand only about a 20 percent loss of blood volume and still recover from an injury.

Signs: With external bleeding, you will see blood on the bird, her cage, and her surroundings. In the case of internal bleeding, the bird may pass bloody droppings or bleed from her nose, mouth, or vent.

What to do: For external bleeding, apply direct pressure. If the bleeding doesn't stop with direct pressure, apply a coagulant, such as styptic powder (for nails and beaks) or cornstarch (for broken feathers and skin injuries). If the bleeding stops, observe the bird to check for more bleeding and signs of shock (see page 102). Call your veterinarian's office if the bird seems weak or if she has lost a lot of blood and arrange to take the bird in for further treatment.

Your conure's breathing should always be regular and clear.

Broken blood feathers can result in bleeding. Blood feathers can break horizontally (across the feather) or vertically (along the feather shaft). Horizontal breaks are more common, and they often result from a bird pulling at a blood feather or an owner accidentally cutting a blood feather while trimming a bird's wings.

In severe cases that do not respond to direct pressure, you may have to remove the feather shaft to stop the bleeding. To do this, grasp the feather shaft as close to the skin as you can with a pair of needle-nosed pliers and pull out the shaft with a swift, steady motion. Apply direct pressure to the skin after you remove the feather shaft.

Breathing Problems

It's an emergency because: Respiratory problems in pet birds can be life-threatening.

Signs: The bird wheezes or clicks while breathing, bobs her tail, breathes with an open mouth, and has discharge from her nares or swelling around her eyes.

What to do: Keep the bird warm, place her in a bathroom with a hot shower running to help her breathe more easily, and call your veterinarian's office.

Burns

It's an emergency because: Birds who are burned severely enough can go into shock and may die.

Signs: A burned bird has reddened skin and burnt or greasy feathers. The bird may also show signs of shock (see page 102).

What to do: Mist the burned area with cool water. Lightly apply antibiotic cream or spray. Do not apply any oily or greasy substances, including butter. If the bird seems shocky or the burn is widespread, contact your veterinarian's office immediately for further instructions.

Concussion

It's an emergency because: A concussion results from a sharp blow to the head that can cause injury to the brain.

Signs: Birds sometimes suffer concussions when they fly into mirrors or windows. They will seem stunned and may go into shock.

What to do: Keep the bird warm, prevent her from hurting herself further, and watch her carefully. Alert your veterinarian's office to the injury.

Cloacal Prolapse

It's an emergency because: The bird's lower intestines, uterus, or cloaca is protruding from the bird's vent.

Signs: The bird has pink, red, brown, or black tissue protruding from her vent.

What to do: Contact your veterinarian's office for immediate care. Your veterinarian can usually reposition the organs.

Egg Binding

It's an emergency because: The egg blocks the hen's excretory system and makes it impossible for her to eliminate. Also, eggs can sometimes break inside the hen, which can lead to infection.

Signs: An egg-bound hen strains to lay eggs unsuccessfully. She becomes fluffed and lethargic, sits on the floor of her cage, may be paralyzed, and may have a swollen abdomen.

Hens will lay eggs even when there are no males around, and that can sometimes lead to problems.

What to do: Keep her warm, because this sometimes helps her pass the egg. Put her and her cage into a warm bathroom with a hot shower running to increase the humidity, which may also help her pass the egg. If your bird doesn't improve within an hour, contact your veterinarian.

Eye Injuries

It's an emergency because: Untreated eye problems can lead to blindness.

Signs: Swollen or pasty eyelids, discharge, cloudy eyeball, and increased rubbing of eye area.

What to do: Examine the eye carefully for foreign bodies. Then contact your veterinarian for instructions.

Fractures

It's an emergency because: A fracture can cause a bird to go into shock. Depending on the type of fracture, infections can also set in.

Signs: Birds most often break bones in their legs, so be on the lookout for a bird who is holding one leg at an odd angle or who isn't putting weight on one leg. Sudden swelling of a leg or wing, or a droopy wing can also indicate fractures.

What to do: Confine the bird to her cage or a small carrier. Don't handle her unnecessarily. Keep her warm and contact your veterinarian.

Frostbite

It's an emergency because: A bird could lose toes or feet to frostbite. She could also go into shock and die.

Signs: The frostbitten area is very cold and dry to the touch and is pale in color.

What to do: Warm up the damaged tissue gradually in a circulating warm (not hot) water bath. Keep the bird warm and contact your veterinarian's office for further instructions.

Inhaled or Eaten Foreign Object

It's an emergency because: Birds can develop serious respiratory or digestive problems from foreign objects in their bodies.

Signs: In the case of inhaled items, symptoms include wheezing and other respiratory problems. In the case of consumed objects, you might have seen your conure playing with a small item that suddenly cannot be found.

What to do: If you suspect that your bird has inhaled or eaten something she shouldn't, contact your veterinarian's office immediately.

Curious conures can get into all kinds of things they should not.

Lead Poisoning

It's an emergency because: Birds can die from lead poisoning.

Signs: A bird with lead poisoning may act depressed or weak. She may be blind, or she may walk in circles at the bottom of her cage. She may regurgitate or pass droppings that resemble tomato juice.

What to do: Contact your avian veterinarian immediately. Lead poisoning requires a quick start to treatment, and the treatment may require several days or weeks to complete successfully.

Overheating

It's an emergency because: High body temperatures can kill a bird.

Signs: An overheated bird will try to make herself thin. She will hold her wings away from her body, open her mouth, and roll her tongue in an attempt to cool herself. Birds don't have sweat glands, so they must try to cool their bodies by exposing as much of their skin's surface as they can to moving air.

> ### C A U T I O N
> **Get the Lead Out**
>
> Lead poisoning is easily prevented by keeping birds away from common sources of lead in the home. These include stained-glass items, leaded paint found in some older homes, fishing weights, drapery weights, and some parrot toys (some are weighted with lead). One item that won't cause lead poisoning is a lead pencil (they're actually graphite).

In an emergency, your bird will rely on you to stay calm and take appropriate action.

What to do: Cool the bird off by putting her in front of a fan (make sure the blades are screened so the bird doesn't injure herself further), by spraying her with cool water, or by having her stand in a bowl of cool water. Let the bird drink cool water if she can (if she can't, offer her cool water with an eyedropper) and contact your veterinarian.

Poisoning

It's an emergency because: Poisons can kill a bird quickly.

Signs: Poisoned birds may suddenly regurgitate, have diarrhea or bloody droppings, and have redness or burns around their mouths. They may also go into convulsions, become paralyzed, or go into shock.

What to do: Put the poison out of your bird's reach. Contact your veterinarian for further instructions. Be prepared to take the poison with you to the vet's office in case he or she needs to contact a poison control center for further information.

Seizures

It's an emergency because: Seizures can indicate a number of serious conditions, including lead poisoning, infections, nutritional deficiency, heat stroke, and epilepsy.

Signs: The bird goes into a seizure that lasts from a few seconds to a minute. Afterward, she seems dazed and may stay on the cage floor for several hours. She may also appear unsteady and won't perch.

What to do: Keep the bird from hurting herself by removing everything you can from her cage. Cover the bird's cage with a towel and darken the room to reduce the bird's stress level. Contact your veterinarian's office immediately for further instructions.

Shock

It's an emergency because: Shock occurs when the bird's circulatory system cannot move the blood supply around the bird's body. This is a serious condition that can lead to death if left untreated.

Can You Catch Avian Flu from Your Bird?

Zoonotic diseases, or diseases that can be passed between animals and people, have gotten a great deal of attention in the first part of the twenty-first century, thanks to diseases such as avian flu, which came to public attention in late 2003 when outbreaks were reported in Asia. Ten countries reported outbreaks in 2004, and fifty-five people worldwide contracted the disease from birds. When this book went to press, the Centers for Disease Control and Prevention had a plan in place to combat avian flu in the event of an outbreak in the United States, and vaccines to combat the disease are under development.

Avian flu is an infectious disease that is caused by Type A strains of the influenza virus. It infects mostly waterfowl, such as ducks, and it can spread to domestic poultry. Wild birds worldwide may be carriers of avian flu. Carrier birds often do not show signs of illness, but they shed the virus through their droppings, nasal secretions, or saliva.

Avian flu is of particular concern to poultry farmers in the United States. Since 1997, about sixteen outbreaks of avian flu have been reported on U.S. poultry farms. These outbreaks were classified as low pathogenic, which means few birds became ill or died. This is in direct contrast to the cases reported in Asia in 2003 and 2004, when thousands of birds became ill or were euthanized to stop the spread of the disease.

People can catch avian flu by coming in contact with the droppings of infected birds or with the birds themselves. This is what happened in Asia during the outbreaks in 2003 and 2004. Symptoms of avian flu in people can range from typical flu-like symptoms, such as fever, cough, sore throat, and muscle aches, to eye infection, pneumonia, and other life-threatening complications. Clinical signs in birds can vary, from birds who show no signs of illness to any of the following: lack of energy and appetite, decreased egg production, soft-shelled or misshapen eggs, nasal discharge, sneezing, a lack of coordination, and loose droppings.

Let me emphasize that it is extremely unlikely that your conure is a carrier of avian flu or that you could catch avian flu from your pet. Avian flu is a greater concern for poultry farmers and bird breeders than it is for the average pet bird owner. I am including information here because the topic has received a lot of attention in television and newspaper reports.

Signs: Shocky birds may act depressed, breathe rapidly, and have a fluffed appearance. If your bird displays these signs in conjunction with a recent accident, suspect shock and take appropriate action.

What to do: Keep your bird warm, cover her cage, and transport her to your veterinarian's office as soon as possible.

Medicating Your Conure

Most bird owners are faced with the prospect of medicating their pets at some point in the birds' lives, and many are not sure whether they can complete the task without hurting their pets. If you have to medicate your pet, your avian veterinarian or veterinary technician should explain the process to you. In the course of the explanation, you should find out how you will be administering the medication, how much of the drug you will be giving your bird, how often the bird needs the medication, and how long the entire course of treatment will last.

This is a safe way to restrain your bird. Make sure not too put much pressure on her breast.

If you find (as I often have) that you've forgotten one or more of these steps after you arrive home, call your vet's office for clarification to make sure your bird receives the follow-up care from you that she needs.

Let's briefly review the most common methods of administering medications to birds (which are discussed completely in *The Complete Bird Owner's Handbook* by Gary A. Gallerstein, DVM). I know from personal experience that all the methods I will describe here do work and are survivable by both bird and owner.

Oral Medication

This is a good route to take with birds who are small, easy to handle, or underweight. The medication is usually given with a plastic syringe, minus the needle, placed in the left side of the bird's mouth and pointed toward the right side of her throat. This route is recommended to ensure that the medication gets into the bird's digestive system and not into her lungs, where aspiration pneumonia can result.

Convalescing Conures

Veterinarian Michael Murray recommends that bird owners keep the following tips in mind when a birds is ill:

- **Keep the bird warm.** You can do this by putting the bird in an empty aquarium with a heating pad under her, by putting a heat lamp near the bird's cage, or by putting a heating pad set on low under the bird's cage in place of the cage tray. Whatever heat source you choose to use, make sure to keep a close eye on your bird so that she doesn't accidentally burn herself on the pad or lamp and doesn't chew on a power cord.
- **Put the bird in a dark, quiet room.** This helps reduce the bird's stress.
- **Put the bird's food in locations that are easy to reach.** Sick birds need to eat, but they may not be able to reach the food in its normal locations in the cage. Sometimes, birds require hand-feeding to keep their calorie consumption steady.
- **Protect the bird from additional injury.** If the convalescing bird is in a clear-sided aquarium, for example, you may want to put a towel over the glass to keep the bird from flying into it.

Medicating a bird's food or offering medicated feed is another effective possibility, but medications added to a bird's water supply are often less effective because sick birds are less likely to drink water, and the medicated water can have an unusual taste that makes the bird less likely to drink it.

Injected Medication

Avian veterinarians consider this the most effective method of medicating birds. Some injection sites—into a vein, beneath the skin, or into a bone—are used by avian veterinarians in the clinic. Bird owners are usually asked to medicate their birds intramuscularly—by injecting medication into the bird's chest muscle. This is the area of the bird's body that has the greatest muscle mass, so it is a good injection site.

Ask your avian veterinarian to demonstrate how to give a bird an injection. Once you are comfortable with the procedure, follow the veterinarian's instructions for injecting your bird. Wrap your bird securely but comfortably in a washcloth or small towel and lay her on your lap with her chest up. Hold her head securely with your thumb and index finger of one hand, and use the other to insert the syringe at about a 45-degree angle under the bird's chest feathers and into the muscle beneath.

You should remember to alternate the side you inject your bird on (say, left in the morning and right in the evening) to ensure that one side doesn't get overinjected and sore. Remain calm and talk to your bird in a soothing tone while you're administering the drugs. Before you both know it, the shot is over and your bird is one step closer to a complete recovery!

Topical Medication

This method, which is far less stressful than injections, provides medication directly to a part of a bird's body. Uses can include medications for eye infections, dry skin on the feet or legs, and sinus problems.

Caring for Older Birds

Your bird may preen a bit less as she ages.

If you've offered your conure a varied, healthy diet, taken her to the vet regularly, clipped her wings faithfully, and kept her environment clean and interesting, chances are your bird will live into old age. You may notice subtle changes in your bird's appearance and habits as she ages. She may molt more erratically and her feathers may grow in more sparsely, or she may seem to preen herself less often.

Although little is known about the nutritional requirements of older pet birds, avian veterinarians Branson W. Ritchie and Greg J. Harrison suggest in their book *Avian Medicine: Principles and Applications* that older pet birds should eat a highly digestible diet that enables a bird to maintain her weight while getting lower levels of proteins, phosphorus, and sodium. They also suggest that this diet contain slightly higher levels of vitamins A, E, B12, thiamin, pyridoxine, zinc, linoleic acid, and lysine, which may help birds cope with the metabolic and digestive changes that come with old age.

When Your Conure Dies

Although conures are relatively long-lived pets, eventually the wonderful relationship between bird and owner ends when the bird dies. Although no one has an easy time accepting the death of a beloved pet, children may have more difficulty with the loss than adults. To help your child cope, consider the following suggestions.

Let your child know that it's okay to feel sad about losing your conure. Encourage your child to draw pictures of the bird, make a collage using photos of your pet or pictures of conures from magazines, write stories or poems about her, or talk about your loss. Also explain to the child that these sad feelings will pass with time. Regardless of a child's age, being honest about the loss of your bird is the best way to help all family members cope with the loss.

While helping their children cope with the death of a pet, parents need to remember that it's okay for adults to feel sad, too. Don't diminish your feelings of loss by saying "It's only a bird." Pets fill important roles in our lives and our families. Whenever we lose someone close to us, we grieve.

Although you may feel as though you never want another bird because of the pain caused by your bird's death, don't let the loss of your conure keep you from owning other birds. Although you can never replace your conure, you may find that you miss having a feathered companion around your house. Some people want a new pet bird almost immediately after suffering a loss, while others want to wait a few weeks or months before bringing another bird home. Maybe you want another conure, or perhaps you'd like to try owning a different species. Discuss bringing home a new pet bird with your family, your avian veterinarian, and bird breeders in your area.

> **Grief Support**
>
> If someone in your family needs to discuss the loss further, the University of California has established a pet loss support hot line. Call (916) 752-4200 for further information. The Delta Society also maintains a directory of pet loss resources. More information about this directory is available by calling (206) 226-7357. Your avian veterinarian's office may know of pet loss support groups in your area, or you may be able to find one by contacting a local animal shelter or SPCA office. Finally, some pet loss support groups are available online through the Internet.

Part III
Enjoying Your Conure

Chapter 9

Your Conure's Behavior

As a new bird owner, you're prob-ably wondering what constitutes normal behavior for your pet and what behaviors indicate that something isn't quite right with your conure.

In this chapter I'll list common normal parrot behaviors. Use them as a starting point to determine what behaviors are normal for your pet bird. Compare them against the list of abnormal behaviors on page 118, which can often indicate illness. If your bird shows any signs of illness, make an appointment with your avian veterinarian for an immediate evaluation. Birds are experts at hiding signs of illness, so by the time a bird looks or acts sick, he is really seriously ill.

As you get to know your pet and as he settles into his new routine in your home, you'll soon learn exactly what behaviors are normal for your pet. It's important for you as a bird owner to learn what is normal for your conure, because your avian veterinarian will often ask for your observations during routine examinations as well as during times of illness.

Common Conure Behaviors

The following common avian behaviors are listed in alphabetical order to help you better understand your new feathered friend.

Attention-Getting

As your conure becomes more settled in your home, don't be surprised if you hear subtle little fluffs coming from under the cage cover first thing in the morning. It's as if your bird is saying, "I hear that you're up. I'm up, too. Don't forget to uncover me and play with me!" Other attention-getting behaviors include gently shaking toys, sneezing, and soft vocalizations.

Bathing

Conures are great bathers and love to be dunked under the water faucet (with a *gentle* stream of water) while sitting on your hand or to stand under a light shower in the kitchen sink. Some birds may even enjoy showering with you, and bird-size shower perches can be purchased or made if you want to try it. If nothing else is available, your conure will try to take a bath in his water bowl. Be sure your pet's bath water is lukewarm before letting your conure take a quick dip, and allow plenty of time for your bird's feathers to dry before he goes to bed to avoid chilling him.

Beak Grinding

If you hear your bird making odd little grinding noises as he's drifting off to sleep, don't be alarmed. Beak grinding is a sign of a contented pet bird, and it's commonly heard as a bird settles in for the night.

Beak Wiping

After a meal, it's common for a conure to wipe his beak against a perch, on your sleeve (if your arm happens to be handy), or on the cage bars to clean it.

Birdie Aerobics

This is how I describe a sudden bout of stretching that all parrots seem prone to. An otherwise calm bird will suddenly grab the cage bars and stretch the wing and leg muscles on one side of his body, or he will raise both wings in imitation of an eagle. Again, this is normal behavior.

Birdnaps

Don't be surprised if you catch your conure taking a little catnap during the day. As long as you see no other indications of illness, such as a loss of appetite or a fluffed-up appearance, there is no need to worry if your pet sleeps during the day.

A little wing stretching is normal for all parrots.

Biting

If your conure bites you in the presence of strangers, he is demonstrating an instinctive flock behavior that is meant to protect you. In the wild, when conures are presented with a threat (such as a stranger), they call to one another to flee, and then may bite at slower-moving members of the flock to hurry them on their way.

If your bird bites you when you are alone, he may simply be testing his environment with his mouth (see "Tasting/Testing Things" on page 118) or he may be demonstrating how well he has trained you. If you react with a lot of dramatic attention (such as speaking in a loud voice or shaking your finger at the bird), the bird will think he has stumbled onto a great game that you will play with him each time he bites you.

Finally, a biting bird may be challenging you for control of his environment. If you want to maintain control of your bird and his environment, look sternly at your pet and use the "up" command (described in chapter 10, "Having Fun with Your Conure") to get the bird onto your hand. This should help keep the biting episodes to a minimum.

Chewing

Chewing helps keep a pet bird's beak in top condition, and it also provides a pet parrot with a way to use up some of his excess energy. Chewing is one of a conure's most common behaviors, which means your pet will need an abundant supply of chewable toys. These can range from empty paper towel rolls to elaborate wooden toys you buy at the pet supply store. If you don't provide a conure with appropriate outlets for his chewing urges, he will find satisfaction in gnawing on your furniture or houseplants. Be sure to supervise your conure when he is out of his cage to prevent him from chewing on inappropriate and potentially harmful things in your home.

Eye Pinning

When a conure sees something that really excites or interests him, you may notice that his pupils contract, expand, and contract again. This is called eye pinning. This action will be easier to see on some conures than on others because some conure species have dark irises that blend in quite well with their pupils.

Fluffing

Fluffing is often a prelude to preening or a tension releaser. If your bird fluffs up, stays fluffed, and resembles a feathered pinecone, however, contact your avian veterinarian for an appointment because fluffed feathers can be an indicator of illness.

Fluffing is one way birds release tension.

Possessiveness

Although it doesn't happen as often with conures as with some other parrot species, a conure can become overly attached to one person in the household, especially if that person is the one who is primarily responsible for his care. Indications of a possessive conure can include biting and other threatening gestures made toward other family members, and pair bonding behavior with the chosen family member.

You can keep your conure from becoming possessive by having all members of the family spend time with your bird from the time you first bring him home. Encourage different members of the family to feed the bird and clean his cage, and make sure all family members play with the bird and socialize with him while he's out of his cage.

Preening

Preening is one of your conure's ways of keeping himself well groomed. You will notice him ruffling and straightening his feathers each day. He will also take oil from the gland at the base of his tail and spread it on the rest of his feathers, so don't be concerned if you see your conure apparently pecking or biting at his tail. Preening, combined with your assistance in bathing and nail and wing clipping, will keep your conure in top shape.

Best bird buddies will form a close bond and may even mimic each other.

If, during molting, your bird seems to remove whole feathers, don't panic. Old, worn feathers are pushed out by incoming new ones, which makes the old feathers loose and easy to remove.

Regurgitating

If you see that your bird is pinning his eyes, bobbing his head, and pumping his neck and crop muscles, he is about to regurgitate some food for you. Birds regurgitate to their mates during breeding season and to their young while raising chicks. It is a mark of great affection, so try not to be too disgusted if your pet starts bringing up his last meal in your honor.

Birds preen to keep themselves well-groomed. Friendly pairs may preen each other.

Resting on One Foot

Do not be alarmed if you see your conure occasionally resting on only one foot. This is normal behavior (the resting foot is often drawn up into the belly feathers). If you see your bird always using both feet to perch, please contact your avian veterinarian because this can indicate a health problem.

Screaming

Well-cared-for conures will vocalize, but birds who feel neglected and have little attention paid to them may become screamers. Once a bird becomes a screamer, it can be a difficult habit to break, particularly because the bird feels rewarded by your negative attention every time he screams. You may not regard your scolding as a reward, but at least the bird gets to see you and to hear from you as you tell him to be quiet.

Sometimes, conures and other parrots are just a little lonesome and in need of reassurance, so they scream to see where their people are. In these cases, simply call back to your bird with "I'm here. Are you okay?" or another reassuring phrase. In many cases, the bird will quiet down quickly after hearing your voice.

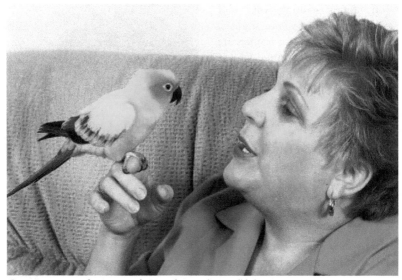

Consistent attention from you—at least two hours a day—will help prevent screaming.

At other times, birds may scream because something in the environment frightens them. In these cases, you will have to work with the bird over time to desensitize him to whatever is scary. If your bird screams at you when you wear a hat, for example, set the hat on a table far away from the bird's cage and gradually (over a period of a few days or a week) bring the hat closer to your bird's cage. Tell your bird how brave he is as the hat gets closer to the cage, and cuddle and pet him to further reward his bravery.

Still other birds scream because they think they have to protect their home and families. This hearkens back to the wild, where parrots alert one another to danger in the area by screaming or calling. In these cases, it's a good idea to check to see that your toaster isn't smoking or there isn't a squirrel on the patio railing before disciplining your helpful watch-parrot.

Sometimes birds will scream when they are tired. In these cases, covering the cage for a few minutes does the trick. If your bird seems to be consistently tired and cranky, you may have to adjust his bedtime. Remember that birds need about twelve hours of sleep a night, and your conure may be disturbed by evening activities, such as the family watching TV or the children doing homework with a bright desk lamp on. A heavier cage cover or relocating the bird to another part of the house at bedtime should do the trick, but remember not to

Stress

Stress can show itself in many ways in your bird's behavior, including shaking, diarrhea, rapid breathing, wing and tail fanning, screaming, feather picking, poor sleeping habits, and loss of appetite.

Over a period of time, stress can harm your conure's health. To prevent your bird from becoming stressed, try to provide him with as normal and regular a routine as possible. Parrots are, for the most part, creatures of habit, and they don't always adapt well to sudden changes in their environment or schedule. But if you do have to change something, talk to your parrot about it first. It may seem crazy, but telling your bird what you're going to do before you do it may actually help reduce his stress.

banish your bird to some far-flung, seldom-used part of your house because this can also cause screaming if the bird feels neglected and forgotten.

Remember to give your bird consistent attention (at least two hours a day), provide him with an interesting environment, complete with a variety of toys and a well-balanced diet, and leave a radio or a television on when you're away to provide background noise, and he shouldn't become a screamer.

Sleeping

Conures are known for two unusual behaviors while sleeping: snuggling under something to sleep, and falling asleep on their backs in their food bowls. You may find your bird napping under a corner of his cage paper (if the cage he lives in doesn't have a grille to keep the bird out of the cage tray). To keep your pet content, give your conure a washcloth, a fuzzy toy, or something else cuddly to snuggle with.

Conures sometimes fall asleep on their backs with their feet in the air. Although this position has an alarming effect on new conure owners, there's nothing wrong with your pet. This is a perfectly comfortable position for a conure to be in.

Abnormal Behaviors

If your conure shows signs of any of the following behaviors, make an appointment with your avian veterinarian because they can indicate illness in a pet bird:

- Sleeping too much
- Sitting with feathers fluffed for long periods of time, even on warm days
- Listlessness
- Lack of appetite
- Regurgitating whole seeds
- Loss of balance or inability to perch
- Feather picking
- Feather chewing

Sneezing

In pet birds, sneezes are classified as either nonproductive or productive. Nonproductive sneezes clear a bird's nares (what we think of as nostrils) and are nothing to worry about. Some birds even stick a claw into their nares to induce a sneeze from time to time, much as a snuff dipper used to take a pinch to produce the same effect. Productive sneezes, on the other hand, produce a discharge and are a cause for concern. If your bird sneezes frequently and you see a discharge from his nares or notice the area around his nares is wet, contact your avian veterinarian immediately to set up an appointment to have your bird's health checked.

Tasting/Testing Things

Birds use their beaks and mouths to explore their world in much the same way people use their hands. For example, don't be surprised if your conure reaches out to tentatively taste or bite your hand before stepping onto it for the first time. Your bird isn't biting you to be mean; he's merely investigating his world and testing the strength of a new perch using the tools he has available.

Birds use their beaks to explore their world and will examine many objects with their mouth.

Vocalization

Many parrots vocalize around sunrise and sunset, which may be a holdover from flock behavior in the wild. The parrots in the flock call to one another to start and end their days. You may notice that your pet conure calls to you when you are out of the room. This may mean he feels lonely or he needs some reassurance from you. Tell him he's fine and that he's being a good bird, and he should settle down and begin playing or eating. If he continues to call to you, however, you may want to check on him to make sure everything is all right.

Yawning

You may notice your conure yawning from time to time or seeming to want to pop his ears by opening his mouth wide and closing it. Some bird experts would say your bird needs more oxygen in his environment and would recommend airing out your bird room (be sure all your window and door screens are secure before opening a window or a sliding glass door to let fresh air in), while other experts would tell you your pet is merely yawning or stretching his muscles. If you see no other signs of illness accompanying the yawning, such as forceful regurgitation or vomiting, you have no cause for concern.

Moving with a Conure

If moving is in your future, your first step should be to acclimate your bird to traveling in the car. Some pet birds take to this new adventure immediately, while others become so stressed out by the trip that they become carsick. Patience and persistence are usually the keys to success if your pet falls into the latter category.

To get your conure used to riding in the car, start by taking his cage (with door and cage tray well secured) out to your car and placing it inside. Make sure your car is cool before you do this, because your conure can suffer heatstroke if you place him in a hot car and leave him there.

When your bird seems comfortable sitting in his cage in your car, place the cage in the back seat, secure it with a seat belt, and take your pet for a short drive, such as around the block. If your bird seems to enjoy the ride (he eats, sings, whistles, talks, and generally acts like nothing is wrong), then you have a willing traveler on your hands. If he seems distressed by the ride (he sits on the floor of his cage shaking, screams, or vomits), then you have a bit of work ahead.

Distressed birds often only need to be conditioned to the idea that car travel can be fun. You can do this by talking to your bird throughout the trip. Praise him for good behavior and reassure him that everything will be fine. Offer special treats and juicy fruits (grapes, apples, or citrus fruit) so that your pet will eat and will also get some moisture.

As your bird becomes accustomed to car travel, gradually increase the length of the trips. When your bird is comfortable with car rides, begin to condition him for the move by packing your car as you would on moving day. If, for example, you plan to place duffel bags near your bird's cage, put the bags and the cage in the back of the car for a practice run before you actually begin the move so your bird can adjust to the size, shape, and color of the bags. A little planning on your part will result in a well-adjusted avian traveler and a reduced stress level for you both.

Before you move, make a final appointment with your bird's veterinarian. Have the bird evaluated, and ask for a health certificate (this may come in handy when crossing state lines). Also ask for a copy of your conure's records that you can take with you, or arrange to have a copy sent to your new address so your bird's new avian veterinarian will know your pet's history.

Once you've settled in your new home, develop a rapport with an avian veterinarian in the area and schedule your conure for a new patient exam. That way, you'll know your bird came through the move with flying colors.

Traveling with Your Bird

When I worked for *Bird Talk*, we often heard from bird owners who wanted to take their pets on vacation and people relocating to another state or country. The advice we gave them about traveling with their bird depended on the owner and their pet. These were some of the questions we asked:

Does the bird like new adventures?

Is there a trusted relative or friend you can leave the bird with while you are away?

Does your avian veterinarian's office offer boarding?

How long will you be gone?

Will you be visiting a foreign country?

If the owners were going on a family vacation, we usually recommended leaving the bird at home in familiar surroundings with his own food, water, and cage or in the care of a trusted friend, relative, pet sitter, or avian veterinarian. We advised this because birds are creatures of habit who like their routines, and because taking birds across state lines or international boundaries is not without risk. Some species are illegal in certain states (Quaker, or monk, parakeets, for example, are believed to pose an agricultural threat to some states because of their hearty appetites), and some foreign countries have lengthy quarantine stays for pet birds. It was our professional opinion that, although it is difficult to leave your bird behind when you travel, it is better for the bird. (Of course, if you're moving, that's a different story!)

If you leave your pet at home while you're away, you have several care options available. First, you can

Some birds are just homebodies and prefer not to travel.

T I P

Find a Pet Sitter

To find an experienced, professional pet sitter in your area, check out the web sites of Pet Sitters International (www.petsit.com) and the National Association of Professional Pet Sitters (www.petsitters.org).

recruit the services of a trusted friend or relative, which is an inexpensive and convenient solution for many pet owners. You can return the pet-sitting favor for your friend or relative when they go out of town.

If your trusted friends and relatives live far away, you can hire a professional pet sitter (many advertise in the Yellow Pages, and some offer additional services, such as picking up mail, watering your plants, and leaving on lights and/or radios to make your home seem occupied while you're gone). If you're not sure about what to look for in a pet sitter, the National Association of Professional Pet Sitters offers the following tips.

- Look for a bonded pet sitter who carries commercial liability insurance.
- Ask for references and for a written description of services and fees.
- Arrange to have the pet sitter come to your home before you leave on your trip to meet the pets and discuss what services you would like them to perform while you're away.
- During the initial interview, evaluate the sitter. Do they seem comfortable with your bird? Do they have experience caring for birds? Do they own birds?
- Ask for a written contract and discuss the availability of vet care (whether they have an existing arrangement with your veterinarian, for example). Inquire about the arrangements the sitter makes in the event of inclement weather or personal illness.
- Discuss the sitter's policy for making sure you have returned home. Should you call them to confirm your arrival, or will they call you?

If the prospect of leaving your bird with a pet sitter doesn't appeal to you, you may be able to board your bird at your avian veterinarian's office. Of course, you'll need to find out whether your vet's office offers boarding services and decide whether you want to risk your bird's health by exposing him to other birds during boarding.

Chapter 10

Having Fun with Your Conure

Now that you've learned the basics of caring for your new conure, it's time to really enjoy your pet's companionship. Try to spend time with your bird each day to make sure her emotional needs for companionship and stimulation are being met. Remember that you and your family are substituting for your conure's flock and that your conure is a very social little bird who needs companionship regularly to feel secure and content in her surroundings.

To make spending time with your pet each day a true pleasure, it's best to train her to follow simple commands that make her easier to handle. This way, you can take your conure with you while you are doing homework, talking on the phone, or watching television. Your bird will benefit from the time spent with you outside her cage, and you will have more time to enjoy her. Whenever your conure is out of her cage, be sure to supervise her carefully to ensure she stays safe and healthy! (See chapter 4, "Home Sweet Home," for tips on household safety.)

Taming Your Conure

Taming a parrot was one of the most popular topics of discussion when I worked at *Bird Talk*, and the discussion continues today among avian behaviorists and their clients in bird club meetings, books and magazine articles, and on the Internet.

The first thing to teach your conure is how to step up onto your hand.

A good first step in taming your conure is getting her to be comfortable around you. To do this, give your bird a bit of warning before you approach her cage. Don't sneak up on her and try not to startle her. Call her name when you walk into the room. Try to be quiet and move slowly around your pet. Keep your hands behind you and reassure the bird that you aren't there to harm her, that everything is all right, and that she's a wonderful conure.

After your bird is comfortable having you in the same room, try placing your hand in her cage as a first step toward taking her out. Just rest your hand in the cage, on the floor, or on a perch and hold it there for a few seconds. Don't be surprised if your bird flutters around and squawks at first at the "intruder."

Do this several times each day, leaving your hand in the cage for slightly longer each day. Within a few days, your conure won't make a fuss about your hand being in her space, and she may come over to investigate this new perch. Do not remove your hand from the birdcage the first time your conure lands on it; just let her get used to perching on your hand.

After your conure has calmly perched on your hand for several days in a row, try to take your hand out of the cage slowly with your bird on it. Some conures will take to this new adventure willingly, while others are reluctant to leave the safety and security of home. (Be sure your bird's wings are clipped, as explained in chapter 7, "Grooming Your Conure," and all doors and windows are secured before taking your bird out of her cage.)

If your bird doesn't seem to like this at all, you can try an alternate taming method. Take the bird out of her cage and into a small room, such as a bathroom, that has been bird-proofed (the toilet lid is down, the shower door is closed, all windows are closed, and the bathroom hasn't been recently cleaned with any cleansers that have strong chemical odors). Sit down on the floor, place your bird in front of you, and begin gently playing with her. Don't be surprised if your bird tries to fly a few times. With clipped wings, however, she won't get very far and will give up trying after a few failed attempts.

Step Up, Step Down

Once you've calmed your conure, see whether you can make perching on your hand a game for your pet. Once she masters perching on your hand, you can teach her to step up by gently pressing your finger up and into the bird's belly. This will cause the bird to step up. As she does so, say "step up" or "up." Before long, your bird will respond to this command without much prompting.

Along with the "up" command, you may want to teach your conure the "down" command. When you put the bird down on her cage or playgym, simply say "down" as she steps off your hand. These two simple commands give you a great deal of control over your bird, because you can say "up" to put an unruly bird back in her cage and you can tell a parrot who needs to go to bed "down" as you put the bird in her cage at night.

After your bird has mastered the "up" and "down" commands, encourage her to climb a "ladder" by moving her from index finger to index finger (the "rungs"). Keep taming sessions short (about ten minutes is the maximum conure attention span) and make it fun so taming is enjoyable for both of you.

Petting

After your bird has become comfortable sitting on your hand, try petting her. Birds seem to like to have their heads, backs, cheek patches, under wing areas, and eye areas (including the closed eyelids) scratched or petted lightly. Quite a few like to have a spot low on their back at the base of their tail (over their preen glands) rubbed. Many birds do not enjoy having their stomachs scratched, although yours may think this is heaven! You'll have to experiment to see where your bird likes to be petted. You'll know you're successful if your bird clicks or grinds her beak, pins her eyes, or settles onto your hand or your lap with a completely relaxed, blissful expression on her face.

Some people may try to tell you that you need to wear gloves while taming your conure to protect yourself from a bite. I recommend against this. A conure generally doesn't bite *that* hard and wearing gloves will only make your hands appear more scary to your bird. If your pet is scared, taming her will take more time and patience on your part, which may make the process less enjoyable for you both.

Toilet Training

Although some people don't believe it, conures and other parrots can be toilet trained so they don't eliminate on their owners. If you want to toilet train your bird, you will have to choose a word or phrase that will mean the act of eliminating to your pet, such as "poop" or "go potty." While you're training your pet to associate the word or phrase with the action, you will have to train yourself to recognize what body language and actions indicate your conure is about to eliminate, such as shifting around or squatting slightly. Use the phrase every time you see your conure eliminate.

When your bird seems to associate "go potty" with eliminating, you can try picking her up and holding her until she starts to shift or squat. Tell the bird to "go potty" while placing her on her cage, where she can eliminate. When she's done, pick your bird up again and praise her for being such a smart bird!

Expect a few accidents while you are both learning this trick, but soon you'll have a toilet-trained bird. You can put on her cage about every twenty minutes or so, give her the command, and expect the bird to eliminate on command.

Toilet training will certainly make it a lot more pleasant to have your conure out and about.

Naughty Conures

Training a conure (or any bird) takes a great deal of time and patience. You must first gain your pet's trust, and then you must ensure you never lose it. To accomplish this, you must be careful not to lose your temper with your bird and *never* hit her. Birds are very sensitive, intelligent creatures who do not deserve to be hit, no matter how you may feel in a moment of anger.

Although parrots are clever creatures, they are not linear cause-and-effect thinkers. If a parrot commits action A (chewing on some molding under your kitchen cabinets, for example), she won't associate reaction B (you yelling at her, locking her in her cage, or otherwise punishing her) with the misbehavior. As a result, most traditional forms of discipline are ineffective with parrots.

So what do you do when your conure misbehaves? Try to catch her in the act. Look at your bird sternly and tell her "no" in a firm voice. If the bird is climbing or chewing on something she shouldn't, remove her from the source of danger and temptation as you tell her "no." If your bird has wound herself up into a screaming banshee, sometimes a short time out in her cage with the cover on (between five and ten minutes will do in most cases) will do wonders to calm her down. Once the screaming stops and the bird has calmed down enough to play quietly, eat, or simply move around her cage, take the cover off to reveal a well-behaved, calm pet.

Talking Birds

One of the most appealing aspects of conure ownership is this species' reputation as talented talkers. Although many conures learn to talk, none of them is

Dr. Irene Pepperberg and Alex

An African Grey parrot named Alex, who is being studied by Irene M. Pepperberg, PhD, at the University of Arizona, has a hundred-word vocabulary, can count to six, and correctly answer questions about the size, shape, color, and number of objects shown him. He can categorize objects, telling a questioner what traits the objects have in common or how they differ. Not bad for a "birdbrain"!

guaranteed to talk. The tips here will help you teach your conure to talk, but please don't be disappointed if your bird never utters a word.

Remember that language, whether it's conure or human, helps members of a species or group communicate. Most baby birds learn the language of their parents because it helps them communicate within their family and their flock. A pet conure raised with people may learn to imitate the sounds she hears her human family make, but if you have more than one conure the birds may find communicating with each other easier and more enjoyable than trying to learn your language.

Most experts say that the best time to teach a conure to talk is between the time she leaves the nest and her first birthday. If you have an adult conure, the chances of her learning to talk are less than if you start with a young bird. Male birds may be more likely to talk, but I have heard of some talkative females, too.

Appreciate your conure for the curious, interesting bird she is, whether she talks or not.

Talking Training Tips

You will be more successful in training a conure to talk if you keep a single pet bird, rather than a pair. Birds kept in pairs or groups are more likely to bond with other birds than with people. By the same token, don't give your bird any toys with mirrors on them if you want the bird to learn to talk, since your bird will think the bird in the mirror is a potential cagemate with whom she can bond.

Start with a young bird, because the younger the bird is, the more likely she is to want to mimic human speech.

Pick one phrase to start with. Keep it short and simple, such as the bird's name. Say the phrase slowly so the bird learns it clearly. Some people teach their conures to talk by rattling off words and phrases quickly, only to be disappointed when the bird repeats them in a blurred jumble that cannot be understood.

Be sure to say the chosen phrase with emphasis and enthusiasm. Birds like drama and seem to learn words that are said emphatically—which may be why some of them pick up bad language so quickly!

A single conure is more likely to talk to you. Groups of conures tend to bond more with one another than with people.

Try to use phrases that make sense in context. For instance, say "good morn-ing" or "hello" when you uncover the bird's cage each day. Say "good-bye" when you leave the room, or ask "want a treat?" when you offer your conure her meals. Phrases that make sense are also more likely to be used by you and other members of your family when conversing with your bird. The more your bird hears an interesting word or phrase, the more likely she is to say that phrase some day.

Don't change the phrase around. If you're teaching your bird to say "hello," for example, don't say "hello" one day, then "hi" the next, followed by "hi, Petey!" (or whatever your bird's name is) another day.

Keep training sessions short. Conure breeders recommend ten- to fifteen-minute sessions.

Train your bird in a quiet area. Think of how distracting it is when someone is trying to talk to you with a radio or a television blaring in the background. It's hard to hear what the other person is saying under those conditions, isn't it? Your conure won't be able to hear you any better or understand what you are trying to accomplish if you try to train her in the midst of noisy distractions. Be sure to keep your conure involved in your family's routine, though, because iso-lating her completely won't help her feel comfortable and part of the family. Remember that a bird needs to feel comfortable in her environment before she will draw attention to herself by talking.

Encouraging Your Conure to Talk

Although conures will make noises in their own language, they are not noted talkers. Some will learn a few phrases if the phrases are interesting to them. To improve your chances of having a talking bird, keep the following tips in mind:

- Start with a single phrase and work with it until the bird learns it.
- Speak in a bright, cheerful voice.
- Keep the training sessions short (between ten and fifteen minutes) and repeat them several times a day.
- Maintain a positive attitude and tone when talking to the bird.
- Be patient.

If your bird talks, consider it a bonus. Don't make speaking ability the prime reason to own a conure, because chances are you'll be disappointed and you'll miss out on a wonderful opportunity to have a great pet!

Be patient with your conure. Stop the sessions if you find you are getting frustrated. Your conure will sense that something is bothering you and will react by becoming bothered herself. This is not an ideal situation for you or your bird. Try to keep your mood upbeat. Smile a lot and praise your pet when she does well!

Graduate to more difficult phrases as your bird masters simple words. Consider keeping a log of the words your bird knows. (This is especially helpful if more than one person will be working with the conure.)

When you aren't talking to your conure, try listening to her. Conures and other birds sometimes mumble to themselves to practice talking as they drift off to sleep. Because your conure may have a small voice, you'll have to listen carefully to hear whether your pet is making progress.

You're probably wondering whether the talking tapes and CDs sold in pet supply stores and through advertisements in bird magazines work. The most realistic answer I can give is "sometimes." Some birds learn from the repetition of the tapes and CDs that, fortunately, have gotten livelier and more interesting in recent years. Other birds benefit from having their owners make tapes of the phrases the bird is currently learning and hearing those tapes when their owners aren't around. I recommend against playing a constant barrage of taped phrases during the day, because the bird is likely to get bored hearing the same thing for hours on end. If she's bored, the bird will be more likely to tune out the tape and the training.

Finally, if your patient, consistent training seems to be going nowhere, you may have to accept the fact that your conure isn't going to talk. Don't be too disappointed if your pet doesn't learn to talk. Most birds don't, and talking ability should never be the primary reason for owning a bird. If you end up with a nontalking pet, continue to love her for the unique creature she is.

The Trick to Training Your Conure

One of the best ways to spend time with your conure is to teach her to do simple tricks. Your bird will come to expect and enjoy the extra attention you give her during training sessions, and you will see a stronger bond develop between you and your bird as the training progresses.

Before you begin to teach your conure tricks, make sure you have the patience and perseverance to undertake training sessions. Birds sometimes behave as we expect them to, but sometimes they want to do what they want to do, and it's up to you not to become frustrated or angry with your pet when she does not behave as you expect. Anger and frustration can damage the relationship you have with your bird, so be sure to be patient and cheerful during each training session.

As you begin to plan what tricks you will teach your conure, notice what your bird likes to do and make it part of her trick training. You will

Trick training is built on patience and trust. Remember, birds are very smart and can learn a wide repertoire of behaviors.

Trick Training Tips

To make the most of your parrot training sessions, keep the following points in mind:

- Know what your bird likes and dislikes. If your bird is naturally playful, she will be a better candidate to learn tricks than a bird who is content to sit on her owner's hand for head scratching.
- Provide several short training sessions each day. Pet birds have short attention spans, and they tend to become cranky if you try to teach them something once you've exceeded that attention span. Ten minutes or less, several times a day, is usually more effective than one longer session.
- Make the sessions fun. Remember that these training sessions are supposed to be enjoyable for both you and your bird, and immediately end any session that is not going well.
- Reward your bird's good behavior with a combination of food treats, verbal praise, petting, or cuddling. If your bird loves to have her nape scratched, for instance, give this area extra attention when your bird performs her trick correctly. This way she will learn to respond to different types of rewards, rather than just waiting for a favorite food treat to come her way.
- Appreciate your bird for the unique individual she is. Love your bird because she is your pet, not because of the tricks she can do. Some birds are natural show-offs; others are more reserved. If you have a quick trick learner, teach the bird tricks and add to her repertoire over time. If your bird doesn't seem to enjoy learning tricks, don't force the issue. Appreciate your bird for her other wonderful qualities and love her as your pet.

soon find it's much easier to expand on one or more of your bird's natural behaviors, and that will make trick training easier and more enjoyable for both of you. For example, some conures like to climb while others enjoy holding their wings in the air and stretching (this can be turned into an eagle pose without too much effort). Still others amuse themselves by using their beaks to examine a wide variety of items in their environment, and you can teach them to touch objects as you name them.

Tricks to Teach Your Conure

Your conure is a bright bird and can learn to perform a wide variety of tricks. Her repertoire of learned behaviors is limited only by your imagination and your patience during the training process. Listed here are some beginning tricks to teach your pet. As your training skills improve, you will undoubtedly come up with some tricks that are unique to you and your bird. Good luck, and remember to have fun!

Ride in a Wagon

A conure who is outgoing and unafraid of new toys or new people is a good candidate to learn to ride in a wagon, or even a radio-controlled car. If your bird is shy, though, she may not enjoy riding in a toy vehicle and you might want to try a different trick instead.

To teach your conure to ride in a wagon, you must first get your bird accustomed to the vehicle. Roll the wagon or drive the car in front of your pet to show her what it will do. Praise the bird if she does not run away from the moving vehicle and reassure her that she will be okay if the vehicle motion seems frightening.

After a few days of short sessions of watching the wagon or car roll by, put your bird in the vehicle. Let her sit in it without moving the wagon. Praise and pet your conure as she sits in the wagon, and continue to get the bird accustomed to the vehicle by letting her sit in it for brief periods over several days.

When your bird seems completely comfortable sitting in the wagon, move it a short distance. Praise your conure for her good behavior if she sits calmly, or comfort and reassure your pet if she seems excited or anxious over the vehicle's movement. Put your bird in the vehicle for short rides several times a day, and gradually increase the length of time spent and distance traveled during the rides.

Nod Your Head

A conure who interacts well with her owner and is unafraid of showing off for strangers is a good candidate to learn to nod her head yes and shake her head no.

To teach your bird to nod her head, hold a small portion of her favorite treat just out of reach of her beak and slowly bob it up and down. Your conure will nod her head as she follows the motion of the treat, trying to catch it with her beak. Give her verbal praise, such as, "Is that a yes?" as she nods, so she will associate the words with the motion.

Yes, I do know how to nod my head.

Practice this trick with the treat and the verbal praise, and gradually increase the praise while eliminating the treat.

To teach your conure to shake her head no, repeat the preceding steps but move the treat side to side instead of up and down, so your bird's head will shake side to side to indicate no. Provide different verbal praise, such as, "Is that a no?" as you move the treat from side to side.

Pose Like an Eagle

A conure who enjoys being petted under her wings is a very good candidate to learn to pose like an eagle. Birds who do not enjoy being petted under their wings can also learn this trick, but training them may take a little longer.

Start your training by gently tickling your conure under each wing tip with your index finger. This will cause your conure to raise her wings. Praise her at this point by saying something like "good eagle, good bird" so your conure will begin to associate the word "eagle" with raising her wings.

Practice the combination of gentle tickling and verbal praise at each training session. Increase the use of verbal praise and decrease the tickling until your conure responds to your words alone.

Play Dead

A conure who enjoys being petted and is willing to be turned over by her owner is a good candidate for learning to play dead. First, you must get your bird accustomed to the feel of your hand on her back as she perches on her cage or playgym. When the bird seems comfortable with your hand on her back, hold her between your hands on her side.

After your conure is used to being held on her side between your hands, move to holding her on her back between your hands. Once she seems content to lie this way, remove the hand you have on your bird's feet or belly, and you have a bird playing dead in your hand!

A friend of mine trained her cockatoo to go to sleep in this way, and he enjoys showing off his trick to her friends. She flips the bird over in her hands, tells him, "night-night," and he responds with a "night-night" of his own. He closes his eyes and she carries him to his cage, where he climbs onto his sleeping perch for the night. She is the only person in her family the bird allows to do this trick—he doesn't seem to think anyone else can get it right!

Your bird must have an incredible amount of trust in you before she will allow you to flip her over onto her back. Lying on her back is not a normal parrot posture. If your conure seems distressed when you flip her onto her back, teach her another trick instead of causing her undue stress by insisting she learn this one.

Appendix

Learning More About
Your Conure

Some Good Books

Alderton, David, *You and Your Pet Bird*, Alfred A. Knopf, 1994.
Coborn, John, *The Professional's Book of Conures*, TFH Publications, 1991.
Forshaw, Joseph, *Parrots of the World*, TFH Publications, 1977.
Rach, Julie, *Why Does My Bird Do That?* Howell Book House, 1998.
Spadafori, Gina, and Brian L. Speer, DVM, *Birds For Dummies*, Wiley, 1999.

About Health Care

Doane, Bonnie Munro, *The Parrot in Health and Illness: An Owner's Guide,* Howell Book House, 1991.
Gallerstein, Gary A., DVM, *The Complete Bird Owner's Handbook,* Avian Publications, 2003.
McCluggage, David, DVM, and Pamela L. Higdon. *Holistic Care for Birds,* Howell Book House, 1999.
Rach, Julie, and Gallerstein, Gary A., DVM, *First Aid for Birds: An Owner's Guide to a Happy Healthy Pet,* Howell Book House, 1998.

About Training

Athan, Mattie Sue, *Guide to a Well-Behaved Parrot*, Barron's, 1993.

Doane, Bonnie Munro and Thomas Qualkinbush, *My Parrot, My Friend*, Howell Book House, 1994.

Grindol, Diane and Tom Roudybush, *Teaching Your Bird to Talk*, Howell Book House, 2003.

Hubbard, Jennifer, *The New Parrot Training Handbook: A Complete Guide to Taming and Training Your Pet Bird*, Parrot Press, 1997.

Magazines

Bird Talk
Monthly magazine devoted to pet bird ownership.
Subscription information: P.O. Box 57347, Boulder, CO 80322-7347
www.birdtalkmagazine.com

Birds USA
Annual magazine aimed at first-time bird owners.
Look for it in your local bookstore or pet supply store.
www.birdtalkmagazine.com

Bird Times
This magazine for pet bird owners is published six times a year.
Subscription information: Pet Publishing, Inc. 7-L Dundas Circle,
Greensboro, NC 27407
www.petpublishing.com/birdtimes/

Online Resources

Bird-specific sites have been cropping up regularly on the Internet. These sites offer pet bird owners the opportunity to share stories about their pets and to trade helpful hints about bird care.

To find an avian veterinarian, visit the **Association of Avian Veterinarians** at www.aav.org. To find a holistic avian veterinarian in your area, visit the **American Holistic Veterinary Medical Association** at www.ahvma.org. Both sites offer ways to search for practitioners in your area.

American Animal Hospital Association
www.healthypet.com

American Veterinary Medical Association
www.avma.org/care4pets/

Conures—You Just Gotta Luv 'Em
www.concentric.net/~conure/conures.shtml

The Conure Ring
www.geocities.com/RainForest/Vines/4545/conures.html

International Conure Association
www3.upatsix.com/ica/

Bird Clubs

The American Federation of Aviculture
P.O. Box 7312
N. Kansas City, MO 64116
www.afabirds.org
Publishes a bimonthly magazine, *The Watchbird*, devoted to bird breeding (all species, not only those kept as pets).

Avicultural Society of America
P.O. Box 5516
Riverside, CA 92517-5517
www.asabirds.org
Publishes a monthly bulletin detailing the society's activities.

Bird Clubs of America
P.O. Box 2005
Yorktown, VA 23692
www.birdclubsofamerica.org

International Aviculturists Society
P.O. Box 341852
Memphis, TN 38184
funnyfarmexotics.com/IAS

National Parrot Association
8 N. Hoffman Lane
Hauppage, NY 11788

Society of Parrot Breeders and Exhibitors
P.O. Box 546
Hollis, NH 03049
www.spbe.org

Other Organizations

ASPCA Animal Poison Control Center
(888) 426-4435
www.aspca.org

Parrot Rehabilitation Society
P.O. Box 6202213
San Diego, CA 92612-0213
www.parrotsociety.org
Rescues and rehabilitates abused and neglected parrots.

United States World Parrot Trust
P.O. Box 341141
Memphis, TN 38184
www.theaviary.com/wpt.shtml
Parrot conservation.

Index

Photo Credits:

Eric Ilasenko: 1, 4–5, 26, 27, 28, 29, 31, 33, 35, 40–41, 42, 48, 59, 60, 63, 72, 73, 78, 79, 81, 82, 86, 87, 90, 93, 95, 98, 102, 108–109, 110, 112, 113, 114, 116, 119, 123, 126, 128, 134

Isabelle Francais: 8–9, 11, 12, 16, 17, 18, 34, 37, 44, 46, 51, 54, 58, 65, 66, 68, 71, 75, 99, 101, 104, 106, 124, 131

Howell Book House: 10

Coleen Meeks Bastys: 19, 24, 121

Lynda Lewis: 20, 21, 22, 115, 129

Cheryl Burns: 25

Alan McManus: 30

Sergei Chebotarev: 32

Karen Weiser: 84

CPSIA information can be obtained
at www.ICGtesting.com
Printed in the USA
LVHW080557270420
654493LV00005B/130

9 781630 260651